"This is the book every church leader is looking for! This book takes the mystery out of building a powerful and effective prayer ministry! Ed has helped our church so much, and I'm excited now to see this important content get into the hands of many hungry leaders!"

—Andy Wood,
Founder and Lead Pastor, Echo Church, San Jose, California

"There is no one on this planet that I trust more and go to when I need advice on how to develop a deep prayer life for myself and my church. Ed is not just a theologian, but an expert practitioner on the subject matter of prayer. *The Praying Church* will give you practical tools and strategy on how to implement a life-giving prayer ministry that ushers in the power of the Holy Spirit. This is a must-read for every pastor and church leader."

—Peter Ahn,
Founder and Lead Pastor, Metro Community Church,
Englewood, New Jersey

"This book is a gift to the church. It is biblical, balanced, and practical. It will help you think through the values that undergird your ministry. And it will give you a road map for implementing the value of prayer in your own life and in your ministry. Read it."

—Jim Masteller,
Founder, The Center for Individual and Family Therapy

"Ed offers a thoughtful theological framework, practical teaching that flows from knowledge gained from years of personal experience fullfilling Christ's call on his life and loving people through the ministry of prayer. This book will equip you for prayer ministry and motivate you in your growth in intimacy with Jesus. Additionally, you will be personally blessed as you read The Praying Church and affirmed in your identity and authority as a beloved child of God."

—Bill and Kristi Gaultiere,
Founders of Soul Shepherding

PRAISE FOR *THE PRAYING CHURCH*

"Our world is desperately in need of supernatural leadership that brings more love, healing, and goodness. Amidst all the brokenness and pain spiritual leaders must learn to live and lead with wholeness. Ed Salas is such a leader. For fifteen years I've walked closely with Ed and watched him from a distance. I've seen how the principles of this book are lived out in his life and carried through his leadership. These practical and powerful words are authentic and crucial for our times. Do yourself a favor. Read these words and put them into practice."

—APRIL L. DIAZ,
Founder and Lead Warrior, Ezer + Co.

"This book can be easily described as 'a treasure map to an amazing prayer life.' I have the honor to call Pastor Ed a spiritual father. His authority in the subject of prayer is evident because it is such a strong part of his life. In a world that is desperate for prayer people, this is a must."

—RODOLFO PEREGRINA G.,
Equipo Pastoral, Vereda Church, Mexico City

"Ed's book is an exciting invitation to all of us to participate with the ministry of Jesus, by being drenched in intimacy with our Father and the Holy Spirit. This book lays out an extensive, but practical sight line into the many aspects of prayer. Prayer team modalities are described to develop safe community within which real change can occur in people's lives. The value of knowing how to start up and sustain a successful prayer ministry at your local church is priceless. The ability to live life within a frame of beauty and power is remarkable. If you want a front row seat to experience what our Father loves doing for his children, namely bringing healing and wholeness to a broken world, this is your book."

—JUDITH SCOTT MAYER,
Pastor of Women's Ministry and Director of Prayer Team,
Watermark Church, Costa Mesa, California

"I've known Ed now for over two decades. He is a man that has grown in his love of God and the way he creatively designs and gifts his children. In this book, Ed shares how we as a collaborative loving team (the church) can engage God, one another, our friends, and the spiritual realm with the unique gifts each of us are given. Ed does this in a way that is refreshing, simple, unintimidating, and approachable. It's a naturally supernatural way that even introverts would love. You'll find this book a welcome primer for those you equip to become more like Jesus."

—DAVE GIBBONS,
Founding Pastor, Newsong Church, Santa Ana, California

"Jesus' disciples were wise to ask him to teach them to pray. Likewise, we are wise to pay attention to those who desire to guide us in the way of prayer. Pastor Ed Salas is one of those guides. The Praying Church should serve as a training manual for those who seek to learn how to participate in the ongoing, redemptive, healing conversation that is prayer. Churches who wish to take prayer ministry seriously must put this book on their required reading list!"

—MICHAEL McNICHOLS,
Affiliate Assistant Professor of Intercultural Studies,
Fuller Theological Seminary

"This book is a must-read! Probably one of the most important topics a follower of Christ could ever write about. Ed's love for prayer and his experience in training people in this area is a gift to churches. He takes a potentially intimidating and complex subject and writes it like it's a conversation from one friend to another. His tone allows the reader to feel safe and curious all at the same time. Ed provides a foundational framework that can easily be adapted into most church communities. A great guidebook!"

—REHANA RODRIGUEZ,
Executive Pastor, Newsong Church, Santa Ana, California

The Praying Church

The Praying Church

*Discovering What the Heart
Longs for Through Prayer*

EDMUND SALAS

foreword by Charles H. Kraft

RESOURCE *Publications* • Eugene, Oregon

THE PRAYING CHURCH
Discovering What the Heart Longs for Through Prayer

Resource Publications
An Imprint of Wipf and Stock Publishers
199 W. 8th Ave., Suite 3
Eugene, OR 97401

www.wipfandstock.com

PAPERBACK ISBN: 978-1-7252-7778-6
HARDCOVER ISBN: 978-1-7252-7779-3
EBOOK ISBN: 978-1-7252-7780-9

Manufactured in the U.S.A.   07/17/20

To each of the prayer team members
that I have had the honor to serve with
over the past twenty-five years since doing prayer in team.
We've had the privilege to sit in the front row to witness the
Father's immense kindness and power to bring people into
freedom and expanded capacity to know more deeply his
blessing and the favor of being his beloved. Together we can
truthfully say,
"It doesn't get any better than this."

Contents

PART FOUR: HEALING PRAYER

PART FIVE: INTERCESSORY PRAYER

PART SIX: PRAYERS FOR THE CHURCH

PART SEVEN: PRINCIPLES OF PRAYER

PART EIGHT: A WORD TO LOCAL CHURCH PASTORS AND LEADERS

Foreword

PRAYER IS PARTNERING WITH God to bring about His Kingdom,
His will on earth as it is in heaven. Praying, then, is the most important thing we get to do as Christians.

Ed Salas has served for fifteen years as Pastor of Spiritual Formation at Newsong Church, a church of 1,200 members in Santa
Ana and Los Angeles, California, and in Bangkok, Thailand. In that
position, he has developed several prayer teams within his church
and led prayer trainings in several other churches in the US and
abroad. In this book, Ed shares with us insights from nearly thirty
years of experience in prayer ministry (including fourteen years at
two other churches).

Basic to Salas' approach is the establishing of prayer teams. He
lists five teams with their functions. The variety of giftings available
in the church can be matched then with the variety of needs. He
labels the teams:

1. Healing Prayer Team that prays for physical, emotional and
   spiritual needs.
2. Encouraging Word Prayer Team that first listens for words
   from the Lord concerning discouragement and prays encouragement and blessing.
3. Intercessors Team that prays specifically for the needs of the
   church and its leaders, staff, programs, departments and all
   else that pertains to the church.
4. The Watch that focuses on specific requests submitted to the
   church for immediate attention.

5. Sunday Prayer Team that makes themselves available at the end of Sunday or other services.

Salas is not worried about the details of finding people to form these teams. He says, "When God stirs in the hearts of leaders to place prayer at the center of all ministry activity, and leaders in turn step out in obedience, He provides the people to serve even if it begins with just a handful."

As for occasions for prayer, Salas lists several that might have been overlooked, such as Consecration Prayer, Commissioning Prayer, Impartation Prayer, and Prayer for Home Cleansing and Blessing.

This is a very helpful book and should be in the hands of every pastor. It is born out of much experience and the desire to help church leaders gain greater ability to work with God to grow His Church and His Kingdom on earth as it is in heaven.

May God bless you, Reader, and enable you to profit in your ministry from applying the insights contained in this book.

Charles H. Kraft
Professor Emeritus, Fuller Theological Seminary

Acknowledgments

DR. CHARLES KRAFT, MY professor and mentor, I am forever grateful to you for wrecking my life (in a good way) and changing my world view about how it actually works in the spiritual realm. You are a pioneer in healing prayer and your voice will be heard through the many people whom you have trained and influenced. Thank you for lending your name to this book.

Stephen Bay, your deep understanding of prayer and so many spiritual matters along with your expertise in writing was beyond helpful in preparing the second draft of this work. We've been in the ministry trenches together for a long time; I am very grateful for our shared partnership and am extremely proud of you.

Han Chua, you are truly what a friend can be and so much more. Thank you for loving me so very well and consistently reminding me that you are there for me. I do not deserve your consistent encouragement and selfless support.

Jan Lynn and Jennifer Bello, you have both used your editing skills to do what I could not have done without you. Thank you for carrying my burden the second mile when I needed it most.

Gary Mayes, the many years of our friendship, occasional beer mentoring, and ministry partnership have forever marked my life, and nothing could ever erase that. My heartfelt thanks to you and Margaret for all of the beautiful memories we've made together.

My friend and mentor, James Waldron. Thank you for your investment in my prayer journey from the beginning to this very day. You will always be my Yoda and mean more to me than you could ever know.

Mark and Jennifer Bello, by your faith and obedience, you took the few loaves of bread and fish that you were given and demonstrated how prayer can turn something small and insignificant into something of great worth to deposit into the lives of many others.

Rick and Courtney, when I needed some help to think through some logistical issues for this book, you came to my rescue. Your special friendship means the world to me.

Dr. Michael McNichols, during our first visit together not so long ago, you wisely encouraged me to reach out to Wipf and Stock to inquire about publishing this book. I am grateful that you pointed me in this direction at a most decisive moment.

Matthew McNabb, I didn't always like it when you asked me how my writing was going, but your loving persistence matched with your consistent friendship was a powerful motivator to simply get it done. I love you, friend.

Each of my *Prayer Shield Partners*, you have my eternal gratitude for the years of prayer coverage that truly makes it possible for all that I do in ministry to happen at a much higher level and for my family to thrive as they do. Your service to me is humbling, and my thoughts of each of you often bring tears of gratitude and joy to my eyes.

My wife Ginny and my sons, Jeremy, Timothy and Trenton, you have made many sacrifices over the years so that I could do what is required for the ministry that I love. Thank you for your love and support and for giving me many reasons to press forward in the calling of my life.

Dave Gibbons, thank you for bestowing your trust and confidence in me. I'm acutely aware that the ethos and culture of every church *always* starts with the leader at the top; I love the community where I am privileged to serve. I am grateful to you for conferring to me the freedom to make a Kingdom contribution which is beyond rewarding and fulfilling to my life.

Introduction

> So we fix our eyes not on what is seen, but on what is un-
> seen, since what is seen is temporary, but what is unseen
> is eternal. (2 Corinthians 4:18 NIV)

As MATERIAL BEINGS LIVING in a material world, it's expected that we would regard what can be seen and touched as the primary reality.

However, if I understand the Apostle Paul correctly, he's telling us that what's *really real* are the things that are eternal and that the eternal are things that *cannot* be seen.

We can't see or touch what is most real. Or can we?

It was over two decades ago that a seminary classmate asked our professor, "Dr. Kraft, how much do you know about the spiritual realm?"

He paused thoughtfully, then answered in the humblest tone imaginable, "About 30 percent."

That's not a very big percentage, I thought to myself. Yet, that's when things started to change for me.

I would hear and see new things and personally experience a healing breakthrough when receiving my own one-hour prayer session. Not only did this forever change every belief and paradigm I had about prayer, it also changed the way I've approached my role as a spiritual formation pastor in the local church ever since.

Since those early days of not knowing what I didn't know, I've arrived at a very significant conclusion: prayer is God's invitation to participate in what he is doing, to live and partner with him at the intersection of the material and the unseen realms.

Having said that with complete sincerity and conviction, I don't claim to have *expertise* about prayer in any of its expressions. (I'm maybe at around 15 percent of knowing what's going on in the spiritual realm.) But after years of being a learner and practitioner of prayer ministries in the local church, I do have a lot of *experience*.

"Experience" can be an interesting word. It might even be a loaded word.

My experience in training, developing, and deploying prayer ministers includes countless false starts and mistakes that you might expect when entering a territory that was woefully uncharted. *The Praying Church: Discovering What the Heart Longs for Through Prayer* represents my ongoing journey of continual learning and discovering anew the transformative power of prayer in the lives of people.

Some of these people have walked with Jesus for most of their lives and would have told you that life was already very good and that ministry, for them, was fruitful and fulfilling.

I can say with confidence that many of these same folks have seen dramatic changes occur when they stepped over the threshold into a revitalized personal prayer life, participating in prayer team ministry that offers a front-row seat to witness God's love and power firsthand as they pray for others.

Indeed, life can no longer be the same when one participates in the life-altering breakthroughs that often occur as a result of the expressions of prayer that we'll discuss in the pages that follow.

For leaders who might be nervous or skeptical about giving serious consideration to fostering an intentional prayer ministry emphasis in your context, please know that I'm not suggesting that any one ministry of prayer become *the* featured ministry of the church.

No. If anything, the opposite is true.

I've found that prayer ministry works best, and flourishes most, when done by a small cadre of whom I like to call "nameless and faceless people"[1]: those who don't seek attention for themselves or have a need for fame; those who love Jesus and love partnering with him in prayer; and those who, when they witness things that only God can do, are more than pleased for all the credit to go to him.

You might relate on some levels to the personal stories in this book and find that the ongoing efforts to cultivate a prayer culture, through various expressions of prayer team ministry in my context, might be helpful in your context as well. I present these pages to you in the prayerful hope that they inspire you to take steps to engage in various expressions of prayer as a normative part of your life, personally as well as in ministry.

Sincerely and affectionately yours,
Ed Salas

---

1. This term was introduced by Sang Kim, a prayer team leader, in the early days of my tenure at Newsong Church. He shared with me and some of the other leaders that he felt this was God's heart for us. This term captured us and was quickly adopted as the vision for our prayer teams and anyone who would minister with us in prayer.

PART ONE

Cultivating a Safe Environment for Prayer

1

Hesitant to Pray

I WAS IN MY midthirties, still in seminary and in my first year of being an associate pastor at a megachurch in Southern California, when I began to observe an unexpected pattern that brought me great concern.

Among the many people who would come to the church office to see me for pastoral counseling, a surprising number of them had been deeply wounded by another person in the context of receiving prayer.

Prayer that was powerful and life changing for individuals, and for entire groups of people, wasn't yet familiar to me in those early days of vocational ministry. All I knew in those days was that my own prayer life was anemic—despite the fact that I'd grown up in a solid, Bible-teaching, evangelical church since the age of ten.

Little did I know that the folks I met who had been damaged in prayer would one day be instrumental in shaping my own personal development, forming core values that would influence how I'd lead ministry teams and a prayer movement in the future.

In order to alter my perspective on prayer and radically transform the way I that I prayed, I had to first learn why so many were hesitant to pray.

What is it about prayer that often triggers a genuine level of anxiety among church leaders, many of whom would prefer not to involve themselves in prayer ministries or even be around "prayer people"? Here are a few thoughts, from my perspective, on why this often happens.

AN ENCOUNTER WITH "SPOOKY PRAYER"

When our middle child was nine years old, he was diagnosed with a brain tumor. For one entire heart-wrenching year, we had to watch our little boy endure difficult, seemingly endless rounds of radiation treatments and chemotherapy.

Early on, some friends of mine offered to come and pray for our son.

Before agreeing to it, I thought it'd be prudent to first discuss this with my wife. I mentioned to her that these friends of mine, who were gifted in prayer, wanted to come and pray for our ailing son. "Would that be OK?" I asked.

Her response was unforgettable: "You know he's very frightened already. I don't want anyone coming over who will scare him even more by praying *spooky prayers.*"

Spooky prayers. When I heard this, I knew *exactly* what she meant.

You probably do, too, unfortunately.

Prayers that sound less like a conversation with our Heavenly Father and more like a shouting match with "the devil."

Prayer that commands illnesses to go to "the pit" or "the lake of fire."

Prayer that would frighten any child (or adult, for that matter).

Have you personally encountered spooky prayer yet? Have you experienced the confusion that ensues when a simple prayer request turns into a harrowing, white-knuckle, roller coaster ride?

Spooky prayer: prayer that can scare others from even *wanting* prayer.

QUESTIONABLE MOTIVES

If you've been around a local church for any length of time, perhaps you've discovered not everyone who wants to pray for others does so without motives that stem from his or her own needs or places of brokenness, such as these:

- The desire to know what's *really* going on in the church (which actually amounts to a kind of spiritual voyeurism);
- The hope of cozying up to the pastor;
- The need for a sense of importance by being a big fish in a small pond; and
- The hunger for fresh fodder for gossip.

I've witnessed all of these on many occasions, and I don't believe I'm being too cynical.

A lead pastor whom I know, who wholeheartedly embraces the power of prayer, is reluctant to have an intercessory prayer team where he serves. The reason? He once felt betrayed by a former prayer leader whom he had trusted and opened his heart to.

Years later, he still hasn't completely worked through his disappointment and grief over that experience.

PRAYER AS THE LAST RESORT

Have you ever noticed that asking for prayer isn't usually the first instinct for most people?

In fact, many turn to prayer only as a last resort. Take the woman in Mark 5:24–26. She had been hemorrhaging blood for twelve years and had used up all of her resources trying to get better.

She was desperate. Coming to Jesus was her last hope.

I've found that many people are like this woman, asking for prayer only *after* they've tried everything else and exhausted all of their resources.

Asking for prayer is their last hope. They've probably reached the depths of desperation by this point.

If this is true, we must remember that many of those who come to us for prayer are deeply hurt.

Disappointed.

Vulnerable.

Easily wounded if they are not well cared for.

It should be no surprise, then, that so many of those who had come to my office for counseling were damaged significantly by someone who had prayed for them.

Prayer ministry, if not done biblically and thoughtfully, can lead to spiritual abuse.

People become hesitant to receive prayer.

Churches become reluctant to even offer prayer ministry.

How do we overcome this apprehension and deal with the emotional barriers built up within us over time?

If you agree that prayer is a way to a deeper understanding of God's heart, and you have the desire to lead a prayer ministry, consider some challenging questions that will certainly come up:

- Why do some of our prayers seem to go unanswered, or at least not answered the way we'd hoped for? What do we do when this happens?

- Is there a correlation between the righteousness of a person and the likelihood of their prayers being answered, based on James 5:16: "The prayer of a righteous person is powerful and effective"? (If there is, we're all in trouble because none of us are righteous, at least not on our own.)

- What about "Ask and it will be given to you" (Matthew 7:7–8)? Do we not see prayers answered because we don't ask enough?

Many of the abuses I've observed in a prayer context occur because those who pray, those who receive prayer, or both, lack a thoughtful, theological framework to explain why some prayers seem to go unanswered.

When prayers "fail"—at least, to human eyes—this can easily lead to finger-pointing. Someone or something *must* be at fault for why prayer didn't work.

The person praying wasn't righteous enough.

The person receiving prayer lacked faith.

The church leadership didn't provide adequate spiritual covering.

I've heard them all. When prayer seems to go unanswered, *someone's* getting thrown under the bus. Better duck for cover.

And so, many have been damaged by faulty thinking about prayer—or not thinking at all.

Here's a *big* suggestion for all church leaders. In order to build a framework for a theology of prayer, we must first come into alignment with God's perspective on what the *ultimate desired outcome for prayer* is.

Is it physical healing?

The Gospels list three accounts of Jesus raising the dead: the son of the widow of Nain (see Luke 7:11–15), Jairus' daughter (see Luke 8:49–56), and Lazarus (see John 11:38–44). Wouldn't we all agree that resurrecting someone from the dead is the greatest healing miracle of them all?

But have you ever met any of these three individuals?

Neither have I.

The reason? All of them died.

Again.

Even the greatest of all healing miracles is but a *temporary solution.*

In addition to healing . . . (wait for it) . . . what if we were to understand that the ultimate desired outcome of prayer is actually greater intimacy with the Heavenly Father?

This outcome, we know, will last for eternity.

How might prayer in the local church be different if we remembered this as the *primary motive* for praying even the boldest prayer of faith?

In the early days of initiating prayer ministry teams, I grew convinced that we had to get this right—that *no one* must be damaged in prayer.

"Do no harm" remains a foundational value for every member of the prayer teams I lead. Additionally, we want every person who receives any type of prayer from us to encounter a kind, generous, and loving Father throughout their prayer experience, regardless of whether or not they receive a miraculous outcome.

Our goal then is to connect people to the heart of God, which can happen whether or not we see a desired healing.

My conviction is that we must embrace intimacy with the Father as the ultimate desired outcome for prayer, especially when asking for God's supernatural intervention.

A thoughtful understanding of the ultimate desired outcome for prayer helps to avoid developing a "goofy" theology for prayer.

SPIRITUAL WARFARE: A DEMON BEHIND EVERY TREE?

Another reason leaders in the church are often hesitant to pray is the topic of spiritual warfare, a potential powder keg of theological controversy and feared disrupter of unity.

Yes, it exists—see Ephesians 6:12—but many church leaders fear that prayer ministries could lead to *everything* becoming about spiritual battles.

Perhaps you know people who constantly search for a spiritual cause to every problem. Every physical ailment or every circumstance that does not go their way is, to them, "spiritual warfare."

Frankly, they get weird when they talk about prayer and other supernatural topics.

It doesn't take long to grow weary of such people.

However, it *is* important to note that while everything *cannot* and *must not* be explained as spiritual warfare, the opposite error would be to conclude that *nothing* involves spiritual warfare.

> For though we live in the world, we do not wage war as the world does. The weapons we fight with are not the weapons of the world. On the contrary, they have divine power to demolish strongholds. (2 Corinthians 10:3–4)

So what are the weapons that we have been given to fight with?

Prayer.

Although we live in the natural realm, otherwise known as the material world, we're spiritual beings who are called to live supernaturally. (We'll cover more of what this means—and doesn't mean—in Chapter 9: *Understanding Spiritual Gifts.*)

Living supernaturally has much to do with being awakened to the reality of the Kingdom of God, which is present here and now, and living in constant awareness of that reality, expressed primarily in practices of prayer.

It's important to note the following:

- Living supernaturally *is not* about sensationalizing ministry activities in the church;

- Living supernaturally does *not* compromise maintaining a safe environment;

- Living supernaturally should *never* compromise biblically-sound ministry practices;

- Living supernaturally does *not* mean that things need to start getting weird; and

- Living supernaturally does *not* mean that people need to start acting weird.

Has all this talk of the supernatural—of demons and spooky prayer—made you even more hesitant to engage in prayer ministry?

I can see how it might.

Churches aren't supposed to be places associated with fear or inflicted pain. Ministries are meant to be life-giving environments promoting spiritual and emotional growth, where people have the opportunity to become all that God intends for them to be.

Communities of faith are meant to be safe places to learn and grow.

Creating this level of safety is the responsibility of leadership, to provide a model and to proactively protect the flock from harm. Jesus held leaders of the temple responsible when he angrily addressed them for what the temple had become, as opposed to what it should have been:

> "It is written," he said to them, "'My house will be called a house of prayer,' but you are making it 'a den of robbers.'"
> (Matthew 21:13)

2

The Church Community as a "Safe Place"

A YOUNG MAN ONCE emailed me to request marriage counseling.

I scheduled an initial visit by phone to first get acquainted, and as we chatted, I learned that he and his wife had been attending a larger church nearby—one that offers an abundance of resources to serve the needs of married couples.

When I asked him if he had sought counseling with a pastor from his own church community, he shared something that broke my heart.

This young man told me that his experiences with the church taught him that there was no guarantee of confidentiality if he and his wife were to seek counseling with one of the staff pastors.

His church community was not a safe place. The pastors were not safe leaders. He would need to look elsewhere for marital help.

Initially, I was shocked at what he reported. Then, the more I reflected on my knowledge of church communities in general, the more I was reminded that the church is not always a safe place—and that leaders in the church are not all safe people.

Perhaps you have a story that supports this same, sad realization.

Creating a safe community is *essential* for prayer ministries to be healthy and gain traction in the local church.

When church leadership does the work required to cultivate safety, this not only honors our Heavenly Father, but over time, it earns the church a reputation for trust and confidence, which so many people need and seek out.

WHY IS SAFETY IN THE CHURCH SO IMPORTANT?

One might think that in an age when people display so much of their personal lives on social media for the world to see, few have anything left to hide.

But the opposite is true.

On social media, we're only invited to see what people want us to see: an image of themselves that they claim as their reality.

The truth is, most people have secrets.

Most people have regrets, perhaps carrying shame for things they've done in the past or may still be doing in the present.

Things they never intend to bring into the light of day.

It takes time to build trust with anyone—even longer to build a trusted prayer ministry in a church community.

A leader I admire once shared his take on the anatomy of trust, saying that "trust is the by-product of confidence, and confidence is the by-product of predictability."[1]

Predictability is crucial in establishing prayer ministry in the church. Confidence in the prayer ministers who are, in a very real sense, God's representatives to a "prayee" (one who is requesting or receiving prayer) is vital because it helps increase one's trust in the prayer event. Trust lays the foundation for an environment in which the Holy Spirit is welcome to do what he does so well and for prayer ministers to partner well with him.

---

1. This was said by Bobb Biehl, an executive mentor and church consultant. Bobb has come to Newsong Church several times and has been extremely helpful when a third-person perspective was needed.

I sometimes liken the prayer room to an operating room where surgery takes place: God is the chief surgeon and invites prayer ministers to be his assistants. At the conclusion of the operation, the patient (or prayee) may feel a bit of discomfort, but it's due to the procedure rather than the pain of the original wounding.[2]

SAFE COMMUNITY BEGINS WITH SAFE LEADERS

A safe leader is a person who acknowledges his or her own pain and brokenness,[3] and can humbly speak of it appropriately, doing the necessary work to address that pain.

Conversely, a leader who denies his or her pain or tries to create an image of perfection is unsafe—a potential danger to others whether they realize it or not.

These summary statements are for you to consider if creating a safe community is a priority and if prayer ministry is to flourish:

1. Senior church leadership establishes safety in the community as a key priority for every staff member and ministry leader;
2. Senior leaders hold themselves to the highest standard of accountability and model what it means to be a safe person;
3. Candidates for future pastoral positions must be able to articulate their own pain and share how they have been working on it, hopefully in a community context; and
4. Leadership at every level in the church is fervently committed to keeping all confidential matters confidential, without exception.

---

2. I first heard the distinction between the two sources of pain from Dr. Charles Kraft.

3. In my experience, this is a non-negotiable! One of the things I most appreciate about Newsong Church is the acknowledgment that every person carries pain and brokenness. This truth is in our church's DNA thanks to our founding pastor, who will occasionally (and appropriately) talk about his own pain *without* doing therapy in front of the entire church. I've noticed that most churches that host recovery groups or have recovery ministries also share this important trait.

Cultivating a sustainable, safe environment in any organization can only happen if it's, first and genuinely, a core value.

Core values must originate at the highest level of senior leadership and be fueled by them to have any chance of real impact, influencing all other levels of leadership in the organization.

3

The Importance of the
Prayer Team Model

BEFORE GOING ANY FURTHER, I want to share the importance of praying with a team whenever possible, no matter what type of prayer you're doing. Here are some reasons why.

- *You can use the multiplicity of giftings present in various team members.* Different people have different strengths and gifts in prayer. It's always advantageous to have several people praying, bringing what the Lord has uniquely gifted them with;

- *Praying in team keeps the focus on the Healer rather than on the individual(s) who are praying.* No one is immune to the sin of pride—this is especially true when you start seeing positive results and healing while praying for others;

- *Praying in team provides each person with a built-in accountability system that helps keep everyone's motives pure when praying for others.* It's natural to form emotional connections with the people we pray for and to experience God's love for his people when we pray together;

- *Having multiple team members provides an opportunity to delegate primary responsibilities to each team member.* For example, the point leader of the team may be well-suited to engage the prayee and determine prayer strategy as guided by the Holy Spirit, allowing the second team member the freedom to intercede on behalf of the prayee and other team members throughout the prayer session;

- *Spiritual power increases when God's people pray the prayer of agreement[1]; and*

- *The team approach provides a necessary space for developing apprentice team members.* In our team system, the apprentice's responsibilities are limited to observing the session, interceding for the prayee, and writing down questions they may have for the post-prayer-session debrief.

A DESCRIPTION OF OUR FIVE TEAMS

At my current church, five different prayer team ministries have emerged over the past fifteen years. Each team provides an opportunity for those who are called to serve in prayer ministry to exercise their gifts in a place that best matches their gifting, personality, and temperament. Each team specializes in a different type of prayer, each of which we will discuss in-depth throughout this book.

Healing Prayer Team. My church calls this team Sola Dei, meaning "only God"—a continual reminder that it is God who heals, not us. Men and women team members (usually two to four members per team) pray for individuals who desire healing for physical, emotional, or spiritual wounding in their lives. This is a Holy Spirit-led prayer process in which team members are trained to pray for the "root causes"[2] of pain at the surface of a person's life.

Encouraging Word Prayer Team. This team prays for one person in a fifteen-minute session that begins with listening prayer on

---

1. I'll unpack the meaning of the principle of agreement in Chapter 18.

2. The concept of targeting the "root causes" of pain is something that I learned from Dr. Charles Kraft. When we visit a medical doctor, we would hope that they treat the root cause of an illness, not just the symptoms. This is the same principle we employ in healing prayer as well.

behalf of that person, then continues with words of encouragement and blessing for the person, in accordance with Paul's explicit instructions for this type of ministry (see 1 Corinthians 14:3).

Intercessors Team. This group of prayer people has a particular calling to pray specifically for the Church: its leaders, staff members, ministry departments, and all moving parts that work together to advance initiatives to reach the global and local community with the gospel of Jesus.

The Watch. The focus of this team of intercessors is to pray for specific prayer requests that are submitted to the church on written cards, online, or by phone. Team members are apprised weekly of new prayer requests, with time-sensitive requests sent out by email as soon as they're received by the team leader. Members of this team like having a list of needs to pray for and are highly energized when they receive praise reports about the requests they've been praying for.

Sunday Prayer Team. These team members make themselves available to pray for individuals at the conclusion of Sunday worship services and other special services throughout the year. This team can come alongside individuals in their moment of need or in their desire to respond to the stirring of Holy Spirit within them. SPT members are comprised of members from our other prayer teams who have completed additional training to serve on this team.

When it comes to forming prayer teams, church leadership needn't worry about having the right people at the right time. In my experience, when God stirs in the hearts of leaders to place prayer at the center of all ministry activity, and leaders in turn step out in obedience, He provides the people to serve even if it begins with just a handful.

PRAYER TEAM MEMBERS: CHARACTER ALWAYS TRUMPS GIFTING

When inviting people to join a prayer team, remember that character *always* trumps gifting.

Here's a story. We had just completed eight weeks of training in an intensive discipleship program we call *Sacred Journey:*

Hearing God's Voice in Everyday Life, which focuses on learning to connect with God on a deeper level. Each member of this group understands that much will be required of them and that there are no guarantees they'll be invited to serve on a ministry team upon completion.

I sent one of the *Sacred Journey* participants, Ivan, an email to invite him to continue his training as an apprentice for our Encouraging Word Prayer Team. I asked him to just let me know if he had any questions or wanted to talk further.

Within a few days, Ivan reached out to chat with me.

We met for coffee several days later. I asked, "What questions can I answer for you?"

He replied, "Ed, don't you know that I have no gifting for this ministry you invited me to?"

I mulled over this for a moment and said, "You're a man of deep character and I love your humility. Trust me on this. I believe that you're going to be terrific in this ministry, but if it turns out it's not for you, no problem whatsoever."

He then accepted reluctantly, though he wasn't fully convinced.

Ivan had demonstrated what I believe is of the utmost importance for serving in prayer ministry: character and humility.

Character and humility cannot be taught. They must be cultivated by individuals over an extended period of time, often through stories of hardship and pain.

Because Ivan was willing to take a risk and step out of his comfort zone, God began to work through him in this ministry. His latent gifting for it began to activate following his willingness to serve and be used by God.

Today, Ivan is one of the strongest members of the team, and his leadership is growing as well. He is dearly loved and respected by everyone who knows him.

Most importantly, Ivan is trusted by our community, and trust is key in establishing a sense of safety.

With so much at stake when someone is entrusted to pray for others with the leadership's stamp of approval, I suggest the following to help identify the best possible candidates for ministry service in prayer:

- *Take the time to get to know potential prayer team members.* This will admittedly require a decent investment of time. Be aware that superior people-skills and apparent *good behavior* can often be misleading. However, with the passage of time, one's true character has no choice but to bubble up to the surface and be revealed.

- *Avoid being overly impressed by either a person's resumé of previous prayer ministry experience or his or her spiritual giftings,* especially if these are offered as reasons to be given a *shortcut* into prayer ministry service.

- *Set expectations early on.* Quality control for prayer ministers happens best when a clear pathway for service is communicated well and applied consistently to every prayer minister candidate.

A VISION STATEMENT FOR PRAYER TEAM MEMBERS

Vision creates a picture of where we're going and what we desire to become in the future.[3] I've developed a simple vision statement that acts as a regular reminder of what is required of every team member at the church where I serve:

We are developing specialized prayer teams of well-trained people who are safe and who are God's instruments of his love, kindness, and grace to those whom we have the honor of ministering to in prayer:

- *Well-trained people,* equipped with the necessary tools to deal with virtually any situation that comes our way in the context of the prayer team in which we serve;

- *Safe people,* who understand what is at stake when someone takes a risk by making themselves vulnerable and requesting prayer—in most cases, from a total stranger; and

---

3. See Proverbs 29:18

- *God's instruments,* who recognize that God works in partnership with his people and are committed to following the lead of the Holy Spirit.

What's the confirmation for being on a prayer team?

In addition to the discernment process that leaders have for inviting new people to serve on a prayer team, each potential prayer team member has a process of discernment as well.

We ask them to prayerfully consider whether or not the following statements are true about them:

1. I believe that prayer is God's invitation to participate in what he is doing at the intersection of the physical and spiritual realm;
2. I welcome continued feedback and coaching for my personal growth and development, and I actively participate as a partner (member) in our church community;
3. I actively cultivate a love relationship with Jesus Christ; and
4. I am willing to serve on the prayer line (Sunday Prayer Team) at the worship service which I *already* attend.

Potential team members are asked if the four statements above are true about themselves. This also helps set clear expectations for ministry team service and confirms that there is mutual agreement. We love welcoming people to our prayer teams who are FAT: Faithful, Available, and Teachable!

4

Establishing Prayer Protocols

So, you've assembled a prayer team? Excellent!

Assembling is one thing, but releasing them to pray will be another.

The next step is to first establish protocols that express the core values as guidelines for prayer team ministry. They will reflect the ethos and theological personality of your ministry context.

Establishing prayer team protocols (or "*good manners*" as a mentor friend calls them) is vital in cultivating a safe environment for prayer ministry.

Every church has its own culture and finds different expressions of prayer to be acceptable or unacceptable. So, this may be a helpful start for adapting protocols that your prayer people can adhere to. Because of the vulnerability of people seeking prayer, do remember to keep in mind the following:

- *Requesting prayer takes courage*—the person requesting prayer, oftentimes, is in pain, confused, or desperate about an important matter; they might have exhausted all other options and are asking for prayer as a *last resort*;

- *Trust is vital*—people can be vulnerable to share sensitive information about themselves in prayer requests if they have trust and confidence in the prayer team; knowing that *every* team member is a trustworthy and well-trained leader will go a long way in building this; and

- *Providing a safe space is essential*—prayees are more likely to be open if they know that you've created a safe space where nothing they share will be shared with others; central to establishing safety is the assurance that prayer team members will not tell anyone else about what is shared during prayer; the implicit assurance of confidentiality is essential.

PREPARING THE PRAYER ENVIRONMENT

Preparation of the physical space where you do ministry will contribute to the overall comfort and effectiveness of the prayer experience.

- Choose an appropriate space for prayer (this is very important). Be sure to pray in a space that is comfortable, quiet, and free from interruptions, where confidentiality for the prayee can be maintained.

- Arrange the seating intentionally. Sit close to the prayee without violating his or her personal space. Keep in mind that personal space is informed by one's own culture of origin.

- Prepare basic supplies. Always have a box of tissues on hand, in view of the prayee and within easy reach for them.

(NOT) TOUCHING A PRAYEE

We generally do not lay hands on prayees or use physical touch to comfort them during prayer sessions. Here are reasons why:

- Touch can become a distraction during a prayer session;

- The pain that the prayee may be feeling might be something that God wishes to heal; the prayee's experience of that pain often provides the optimum opportunity for divine healing to take place;

- The Holy Spirit will provide the comfort that the prayee needs—if only we learn to stay out of the way; and

- Stepping in to comfort a prayee with touch may unintentionally communicate that the prayer team member is not comfortable with the prayee's tears or show of emotion.

CONFIDENTIALITY GUIDELINES

When coming to you for prayer, prayees are opening their lives to you.

They're in a vulnerable place.

Team members are expected to preserve the sacred trust that they've been given. Be sure to let prayees know that the prayer session is confidential but not *secret*. Prayees are free to share whatever they wish if they choose to do so, whereas prayer team members are not.

However, there are exceptions.

Every prayer team member is considered a mandated reporter in my context, so at the onset of every prayer session, we share with prayees that we're required to report anything they share regarding the following:

- Suicidal ideation that includes having a plan and the means to carry it out—this person is in immediate danger;

- Homicidal ideation or behavior; and

- Abuse of children or elderlies.

In short, anything that indicates an immediate danger to self or to others is a cause for concern that must be reported to authorities.[1]

---

1. ALWAYS check with a mental health professional when in doubt or question whether someone's words or behavior should be reported to appropriate authorities.

PRACTICAL MATTERS IN PRAYER

Although prayer is a spiritual act, it occurs at the intersection of the supernatural and the natural. There are practical matters to observe as part of creating a safe place for prayer ministry.

SPEAK APPROPRIATELY:

- Speak loud enough to be heard, but not overheard;
- Avoid long, wordy prayers; keep the prayee engaged as an active participant in the prayer process; don't be afraid of stretches of silence; and
- Always allow time for the prayee to hear, sense, or see what God is saying to him or her personally.

PRACTICE PERSONAL HYGIENE AND DRESS APPROPRIATELY:

- Use breath mints and deodorant to prevent unnecessary distractions; and
- Wear modest, non-distracting clothing.

KEEP YOUR EYES OPEN AND OBSERVE PHYSICAL RESPONSES:

- During a prayer session, it's common for there to be some sort of emotional, and often, physical response; praying with open eyes enables you to observe indications of what God may be doing in the prayee;
- Typical responses may include smiling, nodding the head in agreement, tears, a change in facial expression, and involuntary movement such as fluttering of the eyelids;

- Rightly interpreted, these responses can be helpful guides on how to continue praying, but don't assume to always know what a particular response means;

- Be aware of situations needing your response; for example, a person who is crying could use some tissue, which you should have handy for them to help themselves to; and

- The prayees may exhibit physical indications that they're in the thick of spiritual warfare.

DOS AND DON'TS (IN ALL TYPES OF PRAYER)

Do

- Begin by establishing a rapport with prayees. Establish eye contact and be sure to smile;

- *Always* ask permission before you touch a prayee, even if you already know him or her well;

- Touch very lightly on the shoulder or hold only one hand.

Don't

- Don't hold both hands at once, which becomes restrictive;

- *Don't expose* someone in a way that might embarrass them (i.e., "Are you struggling with [this particular] sin?");

- Don't try to be the solution to their problem or pressing need;

- Don't give counsel or advice (wisdom talk);

- Don't talk about your own problems or challenges;

- Don't chew gum while praying; and

- Don't check your phone or text while praying. (Seriously. This has happened.)

A HELPFUL ABBREVIATION

All of the above values can be summarized by the abbreviation PED.

P—*Permission to touch.* This one speaks for itself. Be aware that touch doesn't always communicate warmth or affection—especially to people who have been victims of physical abuse.

E—*English only.* In some traditions, speaking or praying in a prayer language is acceptable and perhaps even encouraged in a corporate gathering. My *suggestion* is that in gatherings which are open to the public (i.e., Sunday worship services), pray in English or whatever language is commonly spoken by the congregation as to avoid being spooky or confusing to someone who is new to the faith.

D—*Do not expose.* Never, ever embarrass individuals by calling out their sins or shortcomings in life, even if you feel confident that you've received revelation from God. This is a violation of privacy. Nothing good can come from such an act as this.

The things we say, and the way we say them, have power. With our words, we can bless or we can curse (see Romans 12:14).

That's why we need to be thoughtful with our words, even when we're praying in the Spirit.

PART TWO

The Power of Words and Your Spiritual Authority

5

The Power of Words

On a Sunday morning at the end of 2014, a longtime friend and church leader we'll call "Vera" approached me between morning worship services. Her tone was mildly distressed. She wanted help sorting out troubling matters regarding her husband's recent change in behavior.

In recent months, "Peter" had entered a kind of deep funk, feeling dissatisfied with his work despite the fact that he was very accomplished and highly respected in his role at a top-notch university.

Vera went on to tell me that he wasn't connecting well with her or their three children—surprising, as this was historically something that he was particularly good at. In fact, I would have called their marriage a model one thanks to the hard work and intentionality that they both invested in their relationship for as long as I have known them.

As I listened to Vera, a thought flashed in my mind: I remembered that Peter's parents had divorced when he was very young, and he had grown up without any kind of relationship with his father.

I immediately blurted out, "I know exactly what to do!"—something I've never said before, an uncharacteristic response from me.

PUTTING THE PIECES TOGETHER

It was in that same season that I was learning more about the power of blessing than I had ever learned before.

I had been introduced to the writings of an excellent Bible teacher named Craig Hill, who had written a book called *The Ancient Paths*,[1] in which one important teaching revolves around the principle of intentionally blessing others. I learned a short time later that Craig Hill had also written a book called *The Power of a Parent's Blessing*.[2]

Of course, I already knew the story of Jacob and his mother, Rebekah. She created an elaborate plan of deception so that Jacob, her favorite son, could steal his father Isaac's blessing from his older brother, Esau, the firstborn son for whom the blessing was intended (see Genesis 26–27).

Just another Bible story about a dysfunctional family illustrating sinful behavior, right?

Turns out, there was more to the story, which posed a better question that demanded an answer: what did Rebekah and Isaac know about the power of blessing that I didn't?

I had much to learn. The truths I have discovered since then are now changing the trajectory of people's lives toward the heart of the Heavenly Father.

THE CREATIVE POWER OF WORDS

What did God use to bring the entire universe into existence?

Words.

The universe was created when God spoke words (see Genesis 1 and 2). Words have tremendous creative power—the power to bless and the power to curse, to give life as well as to kill.

> Pleasant words are a honeycomb, Sweet to the soul and healing to the bones. (Proverbs 16:24)

1. Hill, "Blessing and Cursing," *Ancient Paths*.
2. Hill, *Power of a Parent's Blessing*, 9–24.

> The tongue has the power of life and death, and those who love it will eat its fruit. (Proverbs 18:21)

> Balak said to Balaam, "What have you done to me? I brought you to curse my enemies, but you have done nothing but bless them!" He answered, "Must I not speak what the Lord puts in my mouth?" (Numbers 23:11–12)

> But no human being can tame the tongue. It is a restless evil, full of deadly poison. With the tongue we praise our Lord and Father, and with it we curse human beings, who have been made in God's likeness. Out of the same mouth come praise and cursing. My brothers and sisters, this should not be. (James 3:8–10)

As image bearers of God, our words also have creative, life-producing power when used in the form of a blessing. But notice what the Apostle Paul writes:

> Bless those who persecute you; bless and do not curse. (Romans 12:14)

Why does Paul instruct us to use words to bless and not curse? Because—sadly—we're capable of doing both!

I've heard too many grievous stories about careless words spoken by parents, grandparents, teachers, pastors, and others in roles of authority who have caused severe emotional and spiritual harm to children who are now adults that continue to carry the effects of those injurious words.

These devastating words are curses, which remain in effect every day of the recipients' lives until those words have been intentionally and systematically removed.

The Lord desires his children to use words not to destroy but to powerfully transform and produce life.

God wants us to bless others with our words.

THE ESSENCE OF A BLESSING

I like Craig Hill's simple definition of what a blessing is: "Speaking into another person what God says about them."[3]

With that definition in mind, it quickly becomes apparent that blessing another person begins in prayer by asking our Heavenly Father some questions:

- What is it that you love so much about this son/daughter of yours?

- How have you been so very pleased with your son/daughter?

- What makes you so proud about this son/daughter of yours?

Notice that you are seeking to enter into the heart and mind of God for the person that you are blessing. Be sure to write down everything that you sense, hear, feel, or see what the Father reveals to you.

Also notice that the questions you ask God aren't related to the person's behavior. On a number of occasions, when I've encouraged parents to bless their children regularly, I've heard the response, "I can't bless my teenage child because I don't agree with the decisions they're making with their life."

Remember, when releasing blessing to another, you're coming into agreement with God as you speak what he says about a person, specifically regarding these points:

- *Original design*—every person on the planet has been planned and is wanted by God, fearfully and wonderfully made (Psalm 139:14);

- *Rightful identity*—every person is known by God, even before He laid the foundations of the world, and claimed as His beloved (Ephesians 1:3–6); and

---

3. From an interview Craig Hill did on the Sid Roth show. Definitely worth watching the segment with Craig as he talks about blessing with a dramatization of a man whose life was dramatically changed after he received a blessing from his 87-year-old father on his 65th birthday: https://youtu.be/oiVVOO4yAUk?t=132

- *God-given destiny*—God has a dream for each person in terms of what they are *becoming*; every child of God has been given real significance and purpose in the world (Romans 8:29–30).

Spoken words of truth that are said in a declarative manner, especially those that reflect the heart of God, have the ability to heal and replace the lies that often plague the minds of so many people.

THE SUPERNATURAL POWER OF BLESSING

Remember Peter, who was raised without a father and never received a blessing? The evening of January 21, 2015, was the birth of what I now refer to as a *blessing ambush*.[4]

I asked Vera to send me a list of the men in Peter's life who love him and also love Jesus.

When I received the list of names and email addresses, I recognized at least half of them. I contacted one whom I knew pretty well, someone who enjoyed hosting events at his home. I explained the blessing ambush that I envisioned for Peter and described what I wanted each of the men to prepare for this event. (For reference, this chapter includes instructions for writing a letter of blessing, and an example of a blessing I wrote for a friend's blessing ambush.)

The evening came for Peter to be blessed.

Our host prepared the most marvelous taco bar with all of the trimmings; it was truly a feast for Peter and his friends to enjoy. As we awaited Peter's arrival, those who were meeting each other for the first time had a chance to get acquainted.

When Peter walked in, he was stunned—almost dazed—to see everyone gathered. He asked what was going on. We simply told him that this night was for him, that it was going to be good, and that he would enjoy it.

---

4. I coined the term *blessing ambush* shortly after the first one, when I realized that this would probably become a very important movement, not just in our church community, but hopefully in other ministry contexts as well. Blessing ambush events are now a regular occurrence for men and women of all ages. We've also held special blessing ambush events for single mothers and their children, usually at the time of their twelfth, sixteenth, or eighteenth birthdays as a rite-of-passage event.

The dining room table was cleared after dinner and we transitioned to the primary reason we were there. I gave a brief set-up for what was to follow and explained the importance of blessing and my expectation that there would be a positive shift in the spiritual realm as a result of the life-giving words given to Peter that evening.

The first guest migrated to the head of the table, took a seat next to Peter, and looked him straight in the eye. When he began to read Peter words of blessing that had been bathed in prayer, it wasn't long before you could hear a pin drop.

I quietly glanced at each of the faces around the table and saw in their expressions a deep sense of love and admiration for the friend they had come to bless.

As each of Peter's friends took turns blessing him, it was apparent that we had all entered into a holy space together. The room had become holy ground.

The evening was stunningly delightful in every way, and what transpired surpassed every hope and expectation that I wanted for my friend Peter.

Most importantly, this blessing event was indeed the beginning of the breakthrough that Vera desperately wanted for her husband.

IT'S NEVER TOO SOON OR TOO LATE

If I could choose but one way to make an impact for the Kingdom, my choice would be for the culture of verbal blessing to catch fire in every local church.

My hope is that no one would go through one's entire life without ever having received a verbal blessing from another who took the time to prayerfully see them through the eyes of our Heavenly Father.

Hopefully, it starts with children being blessed by their parents, as well as other adults in their lives who love Jesus, as a way of life. Did you know that in a practicing Jewish home, the children in the family receive a blessing from their father each week as a part of the sabbath meal?

But, blessing doesn't end with childhood. Blessings need to be released to people throughout their lives. Each blessing has the capability to change the trajectory of a person's life.

Craig Hill identifies seven life-stage blessings, listed here with summaries of what might be at stake in each of these stages and what to bless specifically:[5]

1. *Conception blessing*

- The moment that two cells come together—new life!
- Planned and wanted before the foundations of the earth were laid;
- The gender of the baby affirmed; and
- The family that the Lord specifically selected for them.

2. *In-utero blessing*

- The mother and the baby blessed with peace (shalom);
- The development of each of the organs (heart, brain, etc.);
- The spiritual gifts that have already been deposited; and
- The capacity to one day be in relationship with Jesus.

3. *Birth blessing*

- The presence and joy of Jesus in the delivery room;
- The celebration of the angels;
- Welcoming the baby into the world; and
- Declaration of belonging and being wanted.

---

5. The seven life-stage blessings are taken from Hill, *Power of a Parent's Blessing*, 52. The bullets under each life stage are my personal thoughts/suggestions for opportunities to have blessing released. I added "Adulthood" to the Marriage blessing to make sure that we recognize that single adults require a blessing at this stage as well.

4. Childhood blessing

- Love, affection, and security;
- Provision and trust in the name of *El Shaddai*, meaning "*the one who is more than enough to meet my needs*";
- A life without fear of abandonment; and
- A life of being seen, heard, and respected.

5. Adolescence blessing

- Rightful identity;
- Acceptance;
- Blessing of calling into manhood/womanhood; and
- Blessing into God's destiny for who they are *becoming.*

6. Adulthood/Marriage blessing

- Declaration of manhood/womanhood;
- An invitation to join others in the *circle of men* or *circle of women;*
- Blessing for provision for a suitable helpmate (single person); and
- Blessing of original marriage vows (married person).

7. Old Age blessing

- Declaration of being needed and wanted;
- Admiration;
- Honor; and
- Confirming a life of significance.

THE PROBLEMATIC "ORPHAN SPIRIT"

Over the last fifteen years, I've been serving in a church where the median age of the congregation is approximately twenty-nine.

Here, I've noticed a tragic epidemic of young people who have what I discern is the orphan spirit.

Because these young people haven't always received the blessing that their hearts have longed for, consciously or not, they spend much of their adult lives "wandering in the wilderness" as Esau did after he was denied his long-awaited blessing. There are some predictable characteristics of a person with an orphan spirit:

- Lacking a sense of identity or significance;

- No real sense of belonging or being wanted;

- A sense of hopelessness and purposelessness; and

- Insecurity and lack of self-confidence.

There's something heartbreaking about the pervasive nature of the orphan spirit that runs rampant in many churches today.

Yet, the Bible makes it clear that a child of God is not without a spiritual inheritance and has every reason to know experientially that he or she is loved by a Father who claims each child as his own.

Moreover, it is unnecessary for the orphan spirit to persist when the church releases blessings that reflect the truth of God's Word, as revealed in the Epistle to the Ephesians. As God's children, we are all of the following:

- Known and loved by the Father before the creation (see Ephesians 1:4);

- Claimed by the Father through spiritual adoption (see Ephesians 1:5);

- Given an inheritance of hope and purpose in Christ (see Ephesians 1:11–12); and

- Sealed by the Holy Spirit to be with the Father forever (see Ephesians 1:13–14).

The Apostle John understood the importance of knowing that those who believe in Jesus have been given the status of being God's children.

> Yet to all who did receive him, to those who believed in his name, he gave the right to become children of God. (John 1:12)

> See what great love the Father has lavished on us, that we should be called children of God! And that is what we are! (1 John 3:1a)

The essence of blessing naturally combats the development of the orphan spirit.

PREPARING A BLESSING AMBUSH

If you're planning a blessing ambush, it's a good idea to help those you invite to understand what's going to happen and how to prepare ahead of time (at least a couple of weeks in advance). When I invite people to their first blessing ambush, I make sure to send some basic descriptions and instructions provided below.

COMPONENTS OF A BLESSING

A blessing has two primary components, neither of which has anything to do with a person's behavior.[6] This distinction is important to know because there've been times when a parent has told me, "You don't understand. I can't bless my child. I don't agree with the choices they're making." To all parents, I'd like to say that they can—and must—bless their child regardless of whether or not they agree with their child's behavior. The key to blessing anyone is to keep the focus of the blessing on these two components:

1. *Original design and identity*

Ask the Lord to show you afresh the person's unique and beautiful qualities. Allow your blessing to affirm both what God says and

---

6. Hill, *Power of a Parent's Blessing*, 2.

how He feels about him or her. The psalmist captured this thought when he wrote:

> "I praise you because I am fearfully and wonderfully made; your works are wonderful, I know that full well."
> (Psalm 139:14)

Be sure to reflect the deep love and affection that God has for him or her as you release your blessing to the person:

> "See what great love the Father has lavished on us, that we should be called children of God! And that is what we are!" (1 John 3:1a)

2. God-given destiny

In the heart of every parent is a dream for their children to grow up and go into the world on their own one day. In a similar but even more profound way, Father God has a dream for every one of his children, preceding even the moment of conception.

Destiny reflects God's heart and dreams, focusing not on what one does, but rather, on who they are *becoming*. The Apostle Paul captures destiny's emphasis on *becoming* in his Letter to the Ephesians:

> Praise be to the God and Father of our Lord Jesus Christ, who has blessed us in the heavenly realms with every spiritual blessing in Christ. For he chose us in him before the creation of the world. . . In love he predestined us for adoption to sonship through Jesus Christ, in accordance with his pleasure and will. . . . In him we have redemption through his blood, the forgiveness of sins, in accordance with the riches of God's grace that he lavished on us. . . . In him we were also chosen. . . . You also were included in Christ. . . . You were marked in him with a seal, the promised Holy Spirit, who is a deposit guaranteeing our inheritance . . . to the praise of his glory. (Ephesians 1:3–14, excerpts)

WRITING A LETTER OF BLESSING

Use the following as a guide to write a letter of blessing to be brought to a blessing ambush:

- Begin by asking God to help you see the person *through his eyes*;

- Prayerfully handwrite or type the letter of blessing; this will be something that he or she can hold on to for many years to come;

- Be sure to keep your words *positive and life-giving*;

- Declare, if you wish, that you're proud of them:

   a. Be sure to focus on who the person *is* rather than what they *do*;

   b. Call out what you see in them and what you see God doing in them;

- Allow yourself to be vulnerable and share your love for them.

When verbally speaking your blessing, you may consider this approach:

- Read your letter of blessing while positioning yourself at eye level with the person;

- Bless them *in the first person,* in Jesus' name (e.g., "In Jesus name, I bless you . . ."); and

- Boldly and lovingly call out what you see in the person, and what has been revealed to you, as you see them through the eyes of the Heavenly Father.

Here are some additional thoughts:

- When you release blessing, you have the privilege of deeply affecting someone in a positive way; oftentimes, a blessing can bring healing to a person and even alter the trajectory of his or her life;

- Do all that you can *before* the blessing event to overcome any discomfort you may be feeling; remember, it's about them, not you!

- If you're unable to attend the blessing ambush event but would like to write a letter, send it along with someone who could read it on your behalf.

A SAMPLE BLESSING[7]

Dear Jim,

It has been a special joy in my life that you have become one of the dearest friends of my life over the past two-and-a-half years. It is now my honor and my delight to release blessing to you, which, to the best of my ability, reflects The Father's heart for you—what He sees in you and how He feels about you.

In Jesus' name, I bless you to know who you are, to know your true and rightful identity.

You are Lion Heart. In Jesus' name, I bless you to know who you are at an even deeper level of understanding and experience than you already do. I bless you into a richer understanding of the uniqueness in which Father God has called you out to stand, to serve, and to love as the one He calls His own, His Lion Heart.

You are a true shepherd, a shepherd in the order of your Savior who knows those that belong to Him and who loves and protects those who are entrusted to Him. In Jesus' name, I bless you to walk in the footsteps of the Good Shepherd. Continue to love well and protect those who have been entrusted to you.

I bless you now to hear the words that come from your Father's heart to your heart: "Well done my son. Keep up the good work and keep fighting the good fight."

You are a friend, a truly great friend that provides a safe place in spaces that are not always very safe. In Jesus'

---

7. This is the actual blessing that I wrote for my dear friend Jim Dodgen for his blessing ambush in 2019.

name, I bless your continued impact in the lives of people for whom you provide safety. I bless your life's work to be multiplied even as you seek to raise up young Timothy who will continue the work that you have started.

In Jesus' name, I bless the next assignment that Father is preparing you for and in which He will entrust to you in Colorado. May you once again discover the joy that you have sown throughout your life in the adventures that are to come.

With the love and affection of a friend and brother,
Ed

6

Negative Words
(The Ugly Side of the Coin)

FOR THE SAME REASONS that words of blessing are powerful and life-giving, negative words can be equally powerful but utterly destructive to one's personhood.

These words by others, often spoken in a declarative sense, are called *curses*.

Curses aren't always spoken with the intent to bring harm to another. Most curses are words or phrases used, typically, in anger or annoyance but are especially destructive when spoken by someone in a role of authority over a person's life, which includes parents, teachers, and pastors.

Regardless of the original intent of these words, the harm they can bring should not be underestimated, and when spoken by an authority figure, these words are curses by definition. Here are some examples.

"You'll never amount to anything."
"You're stupid and lazy."
"No one will ever love you."

Perhaps an even bigger problem than the curses from others is the self-curse. This is equally insidious and destructive.

Self-curses are the negative words, phrases, and ruminations that people speak to themselves.

These often act as an internal "script" that informs people how they see themselves and how they feel about themselves. This, in turn, influences their behavior.

Whenever people's view or feelings about themselves are not in alignment with God's, these must be discarded as lies that have come from the enemy, then replaced by the truth of God's Word, which is absolute and final.

The prayer process for renouncing and canceling both curses and self-curses, then replacing lies with truth, includes the following elements:

- Ask the Lord to bring to mind the words spoken to me (curses) or by me (self-curses);

- Renounce and cancel, in Jesus' name, the negative words that have been spoken;

- Forgive each person (or yourself) for speaking those words, then blessing them;

- Ask Father God for healing and to be set free from the influences of the curses from this day forward; and

- Make a conscious decision, as often as necessary, to live not under the influence of those curses or self-curses any longer, with God's help.

Once this process has been completed, I encourage you to ask the following questions with the expectation that the Holy Spirit will answer, usually in the way that you would normally *hear, sense,* or *see* that you're communicating with God:

- Ask, "Father God, what lies have I believed as a result of this curse/self-curse?" (Wait for an answer.)

- Ask, "Father God, what is the truth you wish to give me in exchange?" (Wait for an answer.)

I've found that writing out the truths that are received, and keeping them for future reference, can be an important and helpful tool should old lies and scripts resurface in the future.[1]

The importance of being in lockstep agreement with what God says and how he feels about each of his beloved children lays a solid foundation for what comes next: knowing one's rightful identity in Christ.

1. De Silva and Liebscher, *Sozo,* 107–129. Identifying the lies and replacing them with the truth is an extremely helpful tool.

7

Rightful Identity

HAVING WHAT I LIKE to call a "rightful identity" is an absolute necessity for living a life of abundance which Jesus has promised to those who are his. But there will be opposition:

> The thief comes only to steal and kill and destroy; I have
> come that they may have life, and have it to the full.
> (John 10:10)

Jesus warns his followers that there is a thief who is on assignment to steal, kill, and destroy. In this context, the enemy's goal is to attack, by any means necessary, one's God-given, rightful identity.

Allow me to reference 1999's *The Matrix*. Have you seen it? (The first one. Don't bother with the sequels.) If not, two-decades-old spoiler alert.

The story begins by introducing us to Neo, the hero of the story.

Neo is a regular kind of guy, a computer hacker posing as a programmer. He's approached by a mysterious man in sunglasses, named Morpheus, who tells Neo that he's been living in a world of illusion—The Matrix. He also tells Neo that he's "The One" who can save humanity from extinction. (With me so far?)

Neo doesn't believe any of it at first. He certainly doesn't believe that he is The One.

Yet, with time and the help of Morpheus' friend, Trinity, Neo begins to embrace the possibility that he could be chosen—The One that Morpheus says he is.

You know what happens in the movie as Neo begins to embrace his true identity?

That's right—the special effects get even better!

I submit to you that for us as followers of Jesus to truly experience the spiritual "special effects" we desire (deeper intimacy with the Father, a vibrant prayer life, moving in the power of the Holy Spirit, etc.), we must fully embrace our rightful identity and see ourselves the way the Father in heaven sees us.

The New Testament writers are emphatic that all children of God should know who they truly are and fully embrace what God says about them. The Apostle Paul wrote to the Church at Ephesus:

> For he chose us in him before the creation of the world. . . .
> He predestined us for adoption to sonship through Jesus
> Christ, in accordance with his pleasure and will. . . . In
> him we have redemption through his blood, the forgive-
> ness of sins, in accordance with the riches of God's grace
> that he lavished on us. . . . In him we were also chosen,
> . . . having been predestined according to the plan of him
> who works out everything in conformity with the pur-
> pose of his will. (Ephesians 1:4–12)

A "rightful identity" is one in which a child of God comes into alignment and full agreement with what God says and how He feels about them. In other words, a believer's identity must be defined through the eyes of a loving and gracious God, our Heavenly Father, not through the eyes of ourselves or of others.

No other opinion matters.

No words contrary to that which God has declared may rival what he has said.

Why is having a rightful identity so important?

I am utterly convinced that Satan shudders at the thought of a child of God fully discovering and embracing the depths of what it means to be his beloved.

The reason? God's children hold immense spiritual authority. The forces of darkness are no match for followers of Christ who know who they really are—and live like it.

> For though we live in the world, we do not wage war as the world does. The weapons we fight with are not the weapons of the world. On the contrary, they have divine power to demolish strongholds. We demolish arguments and every pretension that sets itself up against the knowledge of God, and we take captive every thought to make it obedient to Christ. (2 Corinthians 10:3–5)

When believers begin to walk in the awareness of who they really are in Christ, their prayer lives are activated, as God intends.

We can learn much from the life of Moses. Remember what kind of start Moses got off to when the Lord gave him the assignment to free the Hebrew people from slavery in Egypt?

Moses didn't yet know that doing the work of the Kingdom can only be realized when we're in full agreement with God about who we are. So, Moses argued with God and tried to avoid doing what the Lord was asking of him. He said, *"Pardon your servant, Lord. Please send someone else"* (Exodus 4:13).

Notice God's response: "Then the Lord's anger burned against Moses" (Exodus 4:14).

Rough.

I'm guessing it takes a lot to wear out God's patience, to the point where his anger would burn against someone.

Moses came very close to eliminating himself from the very assignment that the Lord had uniquely prepared him to do.

IMPLICATIONS FOR SPIRITUAL WARFARE AND RIGHTFUL IDENTITY

I strongly believe that Christians who are misaligned with what God says about them may be more vulnerable to spiritual attack than they realize. In fact, for most individuals, the biggest battles of al warfare are the ones that take place in the mind.

A predictable strategy of the enemy is to attack God's master-pieces—his children, whom he created—by assaulting them from the inside, in their thoughts and perceptions of their own worthiness for Kingdom usefulness. Consider these points:

- Satan is a master of *identity theft* who has launched an all-out attack to steal, kill, and destroy the believer's rightful identity;

- Because Satan is a liar and a deceiver, he'll manipulate those who live with guilt or shame in order to neutralize their Kingdom-effectiveness; and

- When people carry unhealed wounds from the past, Satan will pervert their persistent pain into low self-esteem and self-hatred.

There is much at stake when it comes to helping God's people know—and fight for—their rightful identity.

Solid biblical teaching, healing prayer, and releasing blessing as a way of life in the Church will foster an environment where people are set free to walk in the fullness of their God-given inheritance.

FROM RIGHTFUL IDENTITY TO SPIRITUAL AUTHORITY

Now we can build on the logical outcomes of knowing who you are and *whose* you are.

Our Heavenly Father is the creator and King of the universe. Take a few moments to internalize this awesome truth. Got it?

If so, begin to tell yourself the awesome truth about who you are: a child of the King.

You are a prince.

You are a princess.

And, as a royal child, you carry an immense amount of spiritual authority to which the Scriptures often give account:

> But you are a chosen people, a royal priesthood, a holy
> nation, God's special possession, that you may declare

the praises of him who called you out of darkness into his wonderful light. (1 Peter 2:9)

You will be a crown of splendor in the Lord's hand, a royal diadem in the hand of your God. (Isaiah 62:3)

Then Jesus came to them and said, "All authority in heaven and on earth has been given to me. Therefore go and make disciples of all nations, baptizing them in the name of the Father and of the Son and of the Holy Spirit, and teaching them to obey everything I have commanded you. And surely I am with you always, to the very end of the age." (Matthew 28:18–20)

You, dear children, are from God and have overcome them, because the one who is in you is greater than the one who is in the world. (1 John 4:4)

For though we live in the world, we do not wage war as the world does. The weapons we fight with are not the weapons of the world. On the contrary, they have divine power to demolish strongholds. (2 Corinthians 10:3–4)

You are royalty. And you have authority.

8

Spiritual Authority

ALL AUTHORITY IS DELEGATED

HERE'S SOMETHING IMPORTANT TO know about authority.

Have you ever been out driving your car and noticed a red light flashing in the rear-view mirror? If so, you probably pulled over as quickly as possible and braced yourself for a ticket. Why? Because you knew that it was a police officer who had the authority to enforce the law—an authority delegated to them by higher powers in the justice system.

All authority that anyone holds has been delegated by someone else.

Because they knew the principle of delegated authority to be true, the chief priests, teachers and elders questioned Jesus about whom he had received his obvious authority from (see Luke 20:2).

In Matthew 8:5-13, the centurion who came to Jesus to request a healing for his servant had a deep understanding of this principle.

> The centurion replied, "Lord, I do not deserve to have
> you come under my roof. But just say the word, and my
> servant will be healed. For I myself am a man under

authority, with soldiers under me. I tell this one, 'Go,' and he goes; and that one, 'Come,' and he comes. I say to my servant, 'Do this,' and he does it." (Matthew 8:8–9)

Jesus was greatly impressed with the centurion's faith, as expressed in the way he understood how authority works in the spiritual realm.

In the same way, our Heavenly Father has chosen to delegate his authority to each of his children. And with that authority comes an open-ended invitation to pray. But not small prayers.

Not anemic prayers.

Big prayers.

Bold prayers.

The writer of Hebrews tells us:

Let us then approach God's throne of grace with confidence, so that we may receive mercy and find grace to help us in our time of need. (Hebrews 4:16)

You can move into the presence of your Heavenly Father with confidence. His throne is full of grace for you.

Firsthand discovery of the spiritual authority that you already possess in Christ will radically transform the way you pray and change the things that you'll pray about. A newfound boldness will ensue within you with the realization of how Father God intends for you to live, as one who has been called to walk in the power of the Holy Spirit.

Any previous fear or hesitation that may have kept you from stepping into the fullness of your rightful identity will dissipate, opening the door to greater intimacy with the Father. You'll delight in the awareness that he wants every part of who you are.

Prayer is life-giving to those who love God and desire to love him more.

LIMITATIONS OF SPIRITUAL AUTHORITY— THE PRINCIPLE OF DOMAIN

When discussing the believer's immense spiritual authority, it's important to include a discussion on the limitations of the spiritual authority that any one of us has.

The issue at hand is that of the *principle of domain.* The question we must always ask is, "Whose domain does this matter fall under?"

To illustrate how domain works in the spiritual realm, we can begin by looking at how it works in the natural realm. Take the place where you reside, for example. Your home is your domain—it belongs to you and your name is on the deed or mortgage.

As an owner, you can pretty much paint your home any color that you'd like. However, if you're a renter, you'll probably find it necessary to get the homeowner's approval before making any changes to the walls. In other words, your authority to choose a paint color is limited by a higher authority, to whom you must defer.

Likewise, if you're a member of a Homeowners Association (HOA), you'll probably have to go through a lengthy approval process before painting your home in a color that you'd like. You can circumvent the HOA approval process, but you risk getting fined—or worse, being forced to repaint your home in an HOA-approved color. In this example, you have willingly submitted your authority to the HOA, because you chose to live under that particular domain.

The same is true of domain in the spiritual realm. A believer has virtually unlimited authority for whatever comes under his or her domain but has limited authority for that which is under the domain of another person or group.

Here's an example from my own life and ministry. Occasionally, I receive invitations from friends who'd like a pastor to offer a prayer of blessing for their new home. I'll often use this as an opportunity to teach on domain by saying the following:

"This is your home—your domain—so ev
pastor, you actually have much more authority to
than I do. So, we can do this in one of two ways: I
bless your own home—and I'd be happy to pray, t

you can choose to delegate your spiritual authority to me to bless your home. Which would you prefer?" (Reminder: all authority is delegated.)

This is a fairly simple example that illustrates how domain works. Here's another one to consider: someone contacts me to ask if I, or any members of the prayer team, would pray for a loved one who is suffering with an illness.

My first question is always the same: "Have *they* requested prayer for their illness or are you acting on your own behalf?"

This question is important because a person's body is his or her domain.

Therefore, when people request prayer for themselves, they are essentially delegating their authority to you so that you can pray for them with greater authority. But, if you're asked to pray for someone who hasn't asked for prayer, or possibly doesn't even want it, you haven't been delegated *any* level of authority.

A note on this topic: there is *much* said in the Bible that encourages us to intercede for others in prayer and to bless others in prayer. You never need to second-guess yourself on this. *We always have the authority to love people, intercede for them, and bless them.* Rest assured that you're in alignment with God's will whenever you are doing those.

> Also, seek the peace and prosperity of the city to which I have carried you into exile. Pray to the Lord for it, because if it prospers, you too will prosper. (Jeremiah 29:7)
>
> I thank my God every time I remember you. In all my prayers for all of you, I always pray with joy. (Philippians 1:3–4)
>
> Bless those who persecute you. (Romans 12:14a)

PART THREE

Encouraging Word Prayer

9

Understanding Spiritual Gifts

My hope is that the following discussion on spiritual gifts (the *charismata*, or gifts of grace) would be helpful in alleviating any misunderstandings about spiritual gifts by showing their original, God-given intent and normative use in the Church.

Understood and used appropriately, each spiritual gift ought to reflect that God gave these to the Church for the *common good* of everyone involved (see 1 Corinthians 12:7).

First Corinthians 12 offers the most comprehensive teaching and listing of spiritual gifts in the New Testament, apparently to address some misunderstandings or misuse of the gifts.

1. An overview of this chapter indicates that what Paul had in mind was to underscore the absolute necessity of *interdependence* among believers in the local church. Paul also reiterates this same message in the Epistle to the Ephesians:

> Instead, speaking the truth in love, we will grow to become in every respect the mature body of him who is the head, that is, Christ. From him the whole body, joined and held together by every supporting ligament, grows and builds itself up in love, as each part does its work. (Ephesians 4:15–16)

2. Another, perhaps secondary, theme for 1 Corinthians 12 is the necessity for *unity* in the local church, needed for it to function in a healthy and holistic manner, which was also a priority of Jesus for his followers (see John 17:20–23);

3. The Holy Spirit alone determines to whom specific spiritual gifts are given; no individual or leader can do this; and

> All these are the work of one and the same Spirit, and he distributes them to each one, just as he determines. (1 Corinthians 12:11)

4. In truth, spiritual gifts are given to the Church in the corporate sense but are *stewarded* by individuals within the local assembly of the Church; with this understanding, it becomes clear that Paul *is not* addressing individuals when he writes:

> Now eagerly desire the greater gifts. And yet I will show you the most excellent way. (1 Corinthians 12:31)

> Follow the way of love and eagerly desire gifts of the Spirit, especially prophecy. (1 Corinthians 14:1)

These verses are accurately understood when read through the lens of an Eastern world view; Paul is writing to the Church at Corinth *corporately.* The church, therefore, is being exhorted to make a request for the full complement of spiritual gifts to be present and operative for the effective, *interdependent functioning* of all its members in order that they may work in unity to fulfill God's Kingdom agenda.

1. The Holy Spirit gives the spiritual gifts of grace for the benefit of everyone in the Church.

> Now to each one the manifestation of the Spirit is given for the common good. (1 Corinthians 12:7)

> *Be keenly aware that a strategic plan of Satan is to neutralize the effectiveness of the Church by making the gifts of the Holy Spirit about anything other than their intended purpose.*
> Whenever there is disunity or schism over spiritual gifts in the Church, the enemy wins (at least temporarily) and the Holy Spirit is grieved.

2. The exercise of spiritual gifts are *simultaneously* an invitation to partner with God and with one another to further God's Kingdom agenda. This proposition can be counter-intuitive to the natural propensity for individuals to work alone, especially anyplace where individualism is celebrated and regarded as desirable.

3. Two common misunderstandings regarding spiritual gifts must be clarified:

   • *Misunderstanding No. 1—spiritual gifts are given as a reward for something that a person did;* nothing could be further from the truth; the "gifts of grace" are given without being earned or merited.

   • *Misunderstanding No. 2—spiritual gifts are evidence of one's advanced spirituality or emotional maturity;* once again, nothing could be further from the truth; the patriarch Joseph was given huge gifting *before* he had the spiritual or emotional maturity to handle it, as evidenced by his boasting of his dreams to his brothers (see Genesis 37:5–11); Paul reminds us that every person remains in the process of sanctification:

   > Until we all reach unity in the faith and in the knowledge of the Son of God and become mature, attaining to the whole measure of the fullness of Christ. Then we will no longer be infants. (Ephesians 4:13–14)

In light of these two points, it would be appropriate to warn against giving too much credit to anyone who has received a particular spiritual gift instead of giving all of the credit—the glory, praise, and worship—to God, the giver of the gifts.

So why would God give extraordinary spiritual gifts to someone who is not yet ready to handle them to steward? What might be his reason?

Based on what we know about God and about how the Church is meant to operate, as revealed in the New Testament, the Church seems to work best when those who are more mature in their faith help those who are less mature in their faith.

We don't expect newborn babies to care for themselves. They need an abundance of help from their parents and other loved ones to do *everything*—to feed them, to comfort them when they cry, and yes, to change their countless dirty diapers.

It's a demanding and messy business to be the parent of an infant. However, as infants grow older, our hope is that they would learn to do more on their own, while they remain under the care and tutelage of others who love them and have knowledge, experience, and wisdom to share with them.

As parents, we look forward to a day in the future when we can "launch" our children into the world as mature, capable adults.

In much the same way, part of what we're about in the local church is the care and nurture of newborns in the faith, a charge that can be extremely demanding and messy.

Teaching newborns—and even those who have been in the faith for a very long time—in a way that is life-giving to them and honors God requires resolve, intentionality, a well-defined process, and leaders who are committed to shepherding them.

In my experience, all of the time and effort needed in this endeavor is well worth the investment and is a source of joy and satisfaction, the fruit of which will last for eternity.

In summary, God intends for the Church to thrive together:

- *A healthy church body reflects our continual need for interdependence;* at no time does any one person "outgrow" the need to participate as an integral part of the organism as a whole (see 1 Corinthians 12:21–25); and

- *The church is a family in which every member can be loved, nurtured, and given a place to learn foundational principles on how to get along and flourish in the world;* leadership in a family context implies certain obligations and responsibilities to contribute to the welfare of others (see Galatians 6:9–11); while with the saints in Thessalonica, the Apostle Paul refers to his own conduct as that of a nursing mother and an encouraging father (see 1 Thessalonians 2:7–12).

SPIRITUAL GIFTS AS A MEANS TO LIVING SUPERNATURALLY

The spiritual gifts God gives to his people are intended for us to live life in a way that is utterly supernatural, vibrant, and exciting. As we grow in our understanding and exercising of spiritual gifts, as God originally intended them to be used, we move closer towards the fulfillment of our unique, Kingdom purpose.

10

Encouraging Word Prayer

PROPHECY, OR SPEAKING PROPHETICALLY, is but one of the spiritual gifts listed in 1 Corinthians 12. If not understood or expressed as God intends, this particular gift can take on a life of its own and open the door to pain and disunity in ministry like no other spiritual gift can.

Over the years, I've learned that the word *prophecy* is a serious trigger word for many people (especially in theologically conservative churches like the one I grew up in) and sometimes for good reason. As discussed earlier, many people have been injured in prayer by those who claim to have received a direct message from God.

It can make one question how representatives of a loving and gracious God can sometimes be so *un*loving, hurtful, and lacking in grace.

But the problem of being unloving, hurtful, and lacking grace is certainly not a new one. We read in Genesis 37 that Jacob's favored son, Joseph, had a God-given ability to see the future in his dreams. Nothing in the text explains how or why Joseph had this particular gift, but it appears that no one in his family questioned that he had a legitimate and reliable supernatural ability.

Joseph created tensions, jealousy, and anger between his brothers and himself with his extraordinary spiritual gift. In addition to the problems that he created, Joseph's deeper issue was that he lacked the necessary emotional maturity and character to use what he had been given without irritating others and alienating himself to the point that his brothers came close to murdering him.

Apparently, God sometimes gives extraordinary spiritual gifting to those who are not ready to handle what has been given to them.

Curious indeed. Later in the chapter, we'll examine some possible reasons why God might choose to do this.

In the New Testament, the Apostle Paul found it necessary to address difficulties with people who were delivering words from God in a manner that misrepresented the heart and mind of God for the people that he loves. Paul needed to lay down some very specific ground rules for the people in the Church of Corinth:

> But the one who prophesies speaks to people for their strengthening, encouraging and comfort. (1 Corinthians 14:3)

The Apostle Paul left nothing to the imagination for what was and wasn't permissible when speaking *prophetically* to another in a church context. The guidelines for what's appropriate are simple, concise and clear.

Prophesying. Speaking words that strengthen.

Words that encourage.

Words that comfort.

Nothing more and nothing less.

THE ENCOURAGING WORD PRAYER TEAM

In the church where I serve, the team ministry of *Encouraging Word Prayer* (EWP) are teams of four to five members each that provide prophetic prayer in fifteen-minute appointments on a monthly basis to *anyone* who wishes to come in.

Just over half of those that come for EWP are a part of our church community, while the rest are those who have come by word of mouth. (Good news travels fast.) We're delighted to be a blessing to all whom the Lord sends us. There's a tremendous sense of joy that comes from serving others in this way.

This may be how the ministry operates now, but I must tell you that it took over two years to get it up and running. Here, I'll describe the process of setting up this particular team ministry and conclude with some key values by which we operate.

- *The original Prophetic Tribe, as we called it back then, of about twenty-five people were invited to meet twice a month on a Friday night, over a period of nine months.* We extended an invitation to men and women of every age who had expressed a desire to know God more deeply and who wanted to expand their capacity to hear God's voice more clearly *for themselves.* No promise or suggestion was made that a ministry role was on the agenda for participation in this group.

- *Each time we met, we used the first hour to share a meal together.* (Have you noticed that you can tell the spiritual maturity of a group by the way they potluck?) We laughed a lot and gradually began sharing life together. After dinner, the next two hours were comprised of teaching, with much interaction together. We developed our own curriculum but the focus was on discipleship. Topics included the ministries of each member of the Trinity, walking in a love relationship with Jesus, cultivating a personal prayer life, and praying for one another.

- *Important note: I did not facilitate or teach the Prophetic Tribe alone.* In fact, my co-leader, Alison, ran point for the group experience while I supported her without abdicating my role as the primary shepherd to our committed participants. The partnership with Alison was born out of friendship and trust. I admire her genuine humility, her love for God's people, and her diehard commitment to walk with others in mutual submission and accountability.

- *Following the nine months of Prophetic Tribe,* it was fairly obvious who finished strong and who had an interest to move forward in ministering to others. An invitation to an apprenticeship group was extended to them for three more months. This included sharing individual life maps, reading a couple of books, and practicing what we were learning with each other. Oh, yes—we ate good food together, too.

- *After three years of Prophetic Tribe training,* a shift was made to condense the duration of the training without sacrificing important content or practicum experiences. With that change we have rebranded the name of our training to *Sacred Journey: Hearing God in Everyday Life.* The prayer team is called the *Encouraging Word Prayer Team.* Over the last eight years, new point leadership has emerged and new team members have joined us while others have moved on to different things.

The Encouraging Word Prayer Team values and guidelines include the following:

- "But the one who prophesies speaks to people for their *strengthening, encouraging* and *comfort.*" (1 Corinthians 14:3);

- Share only what the Lord has given; nothing more, nothing less;

- Do no harm!

- No fates (foretelling any type of future events), no mates (promises of future relationships), no dates (predictions of when something might come to pass);

- Serve others from an overflow of a personal love relationship with Jesus;

- Give God all of the credit;

- Live our lives in community;

- Value mutual submission and mutual accountability; and

- Embrace the honor of being a nameless and faceless people.

AN EXAMPLE OF AN ENCOURAGING WORD

The following is an encouraging word that was recorded by the prayee. Her name is Susan, and she is a point leader in our prayer ministry.

I see the Lord playing pinball and you are the pinball. He is playing the game. He has the full control and knows how much pressure to put, where to send the ball over, in what direction. He is having a lot of fun with you and His desire is for you to trust Him. The goal is to gain as many points as possible. He knows where you will thrive, gain more points.

Teaching is where you are wondering, "Hmm, am I gifted in this? Do I have a platform?" But He is telling you, "You like that. I am all for you. I approve of you." Everything you do for him is perfection to Him. You do not have to prepare for perfection or perform. He knows where you are going to succeed. He wants to set you up for success as a teacher when you speak. He wants to cut down hours of preparation. He is saying "Trust Me to know. Do you trust that I will provide you the words? Do you trust Me to give you, on the spot, what I want you to say that you have not prepared?" Trust Him in His partnership. He is preparing you to receive what He has for you. His notes will be far more and surpass what you have prepared. He'd rather spend time with you.

I see you writing and there is a lot of elegance in your writing, elegance in your journaling when you are writing with the Lord. He does enjoy that. He wants you to spend time in intimacy with Him. . . . You go deep with Him in your writing and journaling with Him. . . . I feel like the Lord is saying, "I can give you all that you are researching and studying in a second. Just interact with Me."

I also hear that you are asking, "How long do I work?" in terms of your profession as a doctor. The Lord wants you to fully grow in that, too. It is not really about the job. He is not giving you a definite answer when to quit, but something about wisdom and discernment that He wants to grow in you in that marketplace. You are a true blessing in wherever you are working. There is spiritual radiance around you when you are at work. You are a blessing and light in the spiritual realm. I am not ignoring your questions on how long I work in the marketplace, what am I doing here? What's the next step? Explore the deeper questions with the Lord. He likes the questions you are asking. "I am not ignoring you. I hear your questions and prayers. Gaining wisdom and blessing other people."

I am hearing, "Obedience." You have been really obedient in your workplace, doing your excellent work. Although it may not be a huge amount of time, He honors you for the commitment you made. You have the freedom to quit but it is more about reward and gaining wisdom. You are gaining more wisdom in managing people. You are getting more opportunity to manage people.

God honors your obedience and commitment.

May you stand firm and confident as a teacher, counselor, as a trainer, as a doctor, as a mom, wife, daughter. You wear many hats. May you enjoy and hit every corner in the pinball and rule and reign in all areas that you can excel. You do not have to choose one or the other. God has given you many talents in abundance in human giftedness. You have a brilliant mind. I bless you to continue to succeed in everything you do, in Jesus name.[1]

Susan offered some feedback as she reflected on this word of encouragement:

I am both encouraged and challenged by this word. I am encouraged because the Lord is giving me His perspective of what He is doing with me as He is growing me in the spirit.

Seeing a big picture is important to me and the Lord knows me so well that He is telling me this to encourage me to keep going and persevere, even if it is not easy. I am also encouraged to know that the Lord enjoys the time I converse with Him through journaling. I have sensed His pleasure during these precious times in the past, but having it confirmed by the word is another level of blessing.

I am also challenged by this word. He is telling me to step out in faith and trust Him in so many ways, both in ministry and in my profession. He has given me wisdom and specific steps to take in order to grow in this area. I am challenged but at the same time grateful and motivated. It is like I just received an instruction manual specifically for me.

—Susan

1. I selected this particular word because it is representative of the types of things that might be said in a typical *Encouraging Word Prayer* session.

QUESTIONS FOR CONSIDERATION

1. *Did this encouraging word meet the criteria of 1 Corinthians 14:3?* Was it at all times either strengthening, encouraging, or comforting?

2. *Does this encouraging word accurately reflect the teaching of Scripture?* Does it in any way contradict the written Word of God, the Bible?

3. *Does this encouraging word honor the ministry values and guidelines for our EWP ministry context?* No fates, no mates, no dates?

PART FOUR

Healing Prayer

11

All Are Broken, All Are Fragmented

A NUMBER OF YEARS ago, I visited with a well-known pastor who has earned a reputation for his innovative style of ministry and prolific writing.

While sharing with me, he described the meaning behind his church's newly redesigned logo. He pointed out that the uneven, multi-colored pieces of what looked like stained glass, surrounding the cross of Christ, represented the true condition of the people that filled the church.

"After all," he pointed out, "we are all broken and fragmented people."[1]

Broken and fragmented.

Do we believe that these are the kind of people who should be in our churches?

If we really *did* believe this, wouldn't we intentionally posture our churches to proactively address the need for healing the brokenness and fragmentation in people's lives?

---

1. The leader quoted is Erwin McManus who, in 1998, graciously gave me some of his time without knowing me previously. As you can see, these words made a lasting impact on my life.

Furthermore, didn't the healing ministry of Christ—curing leprosy, giving sight to the blind, raising the dead (see Matthew 11:1–5)—serve to authenticate his own identity and message?

The fulfillment of the Church's mission must also include the continuing work of Christ, through the Holy Spirit, to bring healing and wholeness to those who need it.

To do this, the Church must embrace the fact that it exists to serve and lead people whose lives are full of the messiness of their own brokenness, of the ongoing consequences of *not* discerning the Shepherd's voice (see Isaiah 53:6). The Church exists to reclaim and restore what thieves and robbers have taken away from God's children.

This realization may just be one of the most important reality checks for the Church today.

The local church is filled with people who need to be brought into healing and wholeness. Many in our ranks *have a past* that they would like to keep hidden beneath a constant, low-grade anxiety, out of fear that they might be discovered for what they may have done in their lives B.C. (before Christ).

But imagine for a moment a local church that made a corporate determination to create the kind of environment where people would come to seek prayer—prayer for the gracious, healing touch of God.

Now imagine that the Church, indwelt and empowered by the Holy Spirit, was actually functioning as the *visible presence of Christ* in the community, who would welcome them with open arms.

Imagine that this same local church actually gained a reputation in its community for being *the* place of life transformation, where genuine love and acceptance was the order of the day. Where, no matter how messed up, jacked up, whacked out, broken down or strung up a person might be—physically, emotionally, or spiritually—that they would know, without a doubt, that they could have an authentic encounter with Jesus of Nazareth through the people of God.

His Church.

Jesus Christ came to save sinners (see 1 Timothy 1:15), heal the sick (see Matthew 4:23), and set the captives free (see Luke 4:18).

Jesus commanded his followers to continue the very same ministry which he modeled (see Matthew 10:8).

Consider the kind of place the Church would be if it took the steps to be prepared and willing to receive those who not only need a Savior, but also a *healer and restorer* for their broken and fragmented lives.

THE LOCAL CHURCH IN THE BUSINESS OF TOTAL LIFE TRANSFORMATION

When the local church intentionally and proactively postures itself to meet people in the messiness of their broken, fragmented lives, then and only then does it have the credibility to be the voice of love and the healing touch of God in their lives as well.

Isn't it increasingly obvious that the question before the Church today is whether or not it will choose to be God's instrument, to echo his shout of the redemptive and reconciliatory message of God's love, found in the Gospel of Jesus Christ?

The local church needs to be a place of healing.

The local church needs to be a place of prayer.

If the Church is going to be the hope of the world in practical terms, it must embrace the reality that each of us is broken and fragmented.

That all of us have a past.

And that all of us are in desperate need of God's miraculous healing so that we might be utterly transformed from the inside out to be his worshippers.

Healing prayer is how it all got started for me. Healing prayer was my introduction to how prayer could change my perspective on how God interacts with his people.

I didn't plan it. I didn't see it coming.

I was taking one seminary course per quarter while working a full-time job, a part-time job, volunteering ten-plus hours a week at our church, and doing my best to be a husband and a dad to two young sons at that time. I just needed a class that would fit my busy life!

While scanning the elective course selections for the upcoming quarter, I noticed a class called *The Role of Healing in World Evangelization*. What? I had no real idea what this course was about, but because it fit my crazy schedule, I registered for it.

What I didn't know at the time was that this class, and the man who taught it, would change my life and ministry forever.

From my finite perspective, all that happened was completely unintentional, but as I look back on that season of my life, I regard it as the time I was ambushed by the Lord to show me that my heart was hungry for more.

There often comes a time in the life of those who love Jesus when they begin to long for something more.

After lecturing for over an hour on the first night of class, my professor and soon-to-be mentor, Dr. Charles Kraft, asked our class if anyone wanted to receive healing prayer for any physical problem they were having.

A young pastor raised his hand and said that his lower back had been in pain. He was brought up front, where Dr. Kraft asked the young man if he could gently touch his back as he prayed. Upon receiving permission to do so, Dr. Kraft prayed what I have fondly referred to as *the boring prayer*.

He didn't raise his voice, change his inflection, or speak in a weird language.

He simply asked God to heal the pain in the pastor's lower back.

After a minute or so, Dr. Kraft finished praying and asked the young pastor if there was any improvement or pain relief.

The young pastor, perhaps trying to be hopeful, mumbled a few words that it might have felt a little better, to which Dr. Kraft responded, "If it doesn't feel better, you don't need to say that it does."

With that, he turned to the class and said, "I don't know why, but it doesn't always work." He then told the pastor to take his seat.

And that's when he had me. I knew in that moment I could trust him.

I had to learn more.

Until learning what I did from Dr. Kraft, my limited experience with healing prayer was what I had seen on television, which was, to me, outlandish sensationalism: yelling, speaking in indiscernible languages (or tongues), shaking, people falling on the ground, crying, shouting, and more.

It certainly isn't my place to say that God doesn't use various expressions of prayer, including that which I've described above, to heal. What I can say with confidence, however, is that I never thought that someone like me, who was raised in a conservative, rather unemotional (bordering on cerebral) church, would stick around to participate in this expression of prayer.

As I discovered in this transformative season of my life, nothing has changed since the days of Jesus, as recorded in the gospel accounts, or the Apostles, as recorded in the Epistles. It took a thoughtful, emotionally low-key, Scripture-centered approach to get past my volitional barriers and discover what I hadn't known throughout most of my adult life—that God loves to heal the sick and loves to use his people in the healing process.

It's true that not everyone who receives healing prayer gets healed. God is absolutely not obligated to heal; there are no formulas that force the healing hand of God when we pray.

Beware of slipping into the trap of "magical thinking," i.e., believing that one can effect desired results by praying a specific way, not unlike an incantation. Magical thinking can easily occur if one isn't keenly aware that the ultimate desired outcome for healing prayer in not the healing itself, but rather, greater intimacy with the Father.

However, is there anything we need to understand about how prayer works and affects the spiritual realm that could help increase the effectiveness of our prayers?

Yes, for sure.

TWO PARADIGMS FOR UNDERSTANDING HEALING PRAYER

Two visuals help us better understand the relationship between the three parts of human beings that often require God's healing touch: our physical bodies, our emotions, and the aspect of us that we identify as our spiritual selves.[2]

2. The paradigms come straight from one of Dr. Kraft's lectures that I heard

In Figure 1, note that the physical, emotional, and spiritual aspects of human beings appear to be separated and unrelated to one another when depicted horizontally.

Figure 1: Horizontal (traditional) understanding

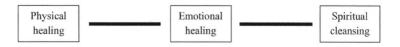

But notice in Figure 2 that when depicted vertically, the physical, emotional, and spiritual aspects of a person appear connected and related to one another. This is especially helpful when trying to determine what might be the original *source* or *root cause* of a specific point of pain.

Figure 2: Vertical (preferred) understanding

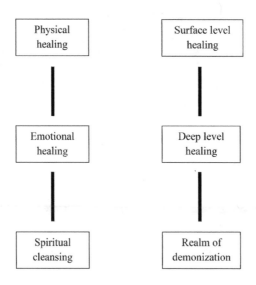

---

while taking his healing prayer course, *The Role of Healing Ministry in World Evangelization*, Fuller Theological Seminary, 1996.

A PHYSICAL AND EMOTIONAL CONNECTION

Shortly after learning the connection between the physical, emotional and spiritual facets of human beings, I went to pray for someone that I had known for many years.

My friend "David" was experiencing severe abdominal pain. When I asked him how long it had been, expecting him to say perhaps a week or two, I was shocked to hear that the intermittent pain had lasted more than thirty years!

Thanks to the prayer training I had recently received, I considered possible root causes of any pain without assuming that it was merely physical.

I asked David if he'd be willing to share what was going on in his life when the pain began three decades prior. He opened up about some of the things he was doing at the time, which he described as "sinful" and "shameful." He'd been wracked with guilt ever since.

The prayer strategy I chose did not focus on his pressing symptoms—the abdominal pain. Instead, I started leading him to willingly receive God's forgiveness and find freedom from the shame and guilt of his past choices.

Notice that the prayer strategy focused on the *root cause* rather than on the *surface symptoms* alone. The result of our prayer time was complete restoration of his relationship with Father God and complete healing of his abdominal pain.

WHAT DOES THE MEDICAL COMMUNITY HAVE TO SAY?

As Dr. Susanne Babbel, a psychologist specializing in trauma and depression, writes in *Psychology Today*:

> "Studies have shown that chronic pain might not only be caused by physical injury but also by stress and emotional issues." She goes on, "Often, physical pain functions to warn a person that there is still emotional work to be done."

Other members of the medical community also support the notion that physical ailments have their root cause in the emotional arena.[3]

A PHYSICAL, EMOTIONAL, AND SPIRITUAL CONNECTION

The following story is a composite of many similar examples of people who have received healing prayer over the years.

"Amanda" reached out via email, urgently requesting help for recurring nightmares that had terrified her most nights. Her dreams always included dark creatures that meant to do her harm. She'd often wake up screaming after being chased by these malevolent beings.

I asked Amanda if I could ask her questions about any occult involvement that she or any of her family members may have had in the past. She told me about her deceased, maternal grandmother who was a "healer" that had gained a reputation for helping those who'd come to be treated for physical ailments. Amanda recounted a time when, as a little girl, she was taken to her grandmother by her mother when she was sick with fever. She received her grandmother's non-traditional, homemade remedies, which were administered with words spoken in a language unfamiliar to her.

I suggested to Amanda that her grandmother was likely practicing some form of witchcraft. Amanda wasn't surprised by this possibility. She recalled that some of those who had come to her grandmother for healing would call her *La Bruja*—the witch.

I asked Amanda if she'd be willing to break all ties of witchcraft that were introduced to her through both her grandmother and her mother.

Amanda agreed. She wanted no part of whatever was behind her grandmother's "healing" practices.

I walked Amanda through prayers of renunciation for witchcraft, spells, incantations, spiritism, and all forms of occult healing

3. For Dr. Babbel's quote and other examples, see https://www.huffpost.com/entry/the-incredible-way-your-e_b_7464472

and occult practices. Amanda also forgave her family members for introducing her to the realm of the demonic.

Afterwards, I chatted with Amanda about the immense spiritual authority she possesses as a beloved child of God and gave her a prayer to spiritually cleanse her home. A few days later, she reported that the nightmares had completely stopped. Amanda could sleep peacefully once again.

SUMMARY OF AMANDA'S STORY

This case illustrates how the physical, emotional, and spiritual aspects of human beings are inseparably connected.

Amanda's physical manifestations (the nightmares) and emotional responses (her fear and terror) could be addressed when her family history and personal experiences with spirituality were revealed.

In her childhood, Amanda had participated in the occult practices of her grandmother, but not by her own volition or intent; she did what was required of her by her mother and grandmother. Unfortunately, this was enough to open doors to the dark side of the spiritual realm and made Amanda vulnerable to the frightful intimidation tactics of the enemy.

As an adult who has a relationship with Jesus Christ, Amanda holds the ability to exercise her own will and appropriate the spiritual authority that she has in Christ to break all ties with the enemy and close all doors to spiritual darkness.

You also have this spiritual authority. You are a child of God.

DEVELOPING A HEALING PRAYER PHILOSOPHY

In early 2013, a church in the Pacific Northwest invited me to do a healing prayer training workshop.

On the eve of the workshop, I was asked to meet with senior pastoral leadership and key leaders to give an overview of my philosophy of healing prayer. I was convinced that if my philosophy didn't meet with the leadership's approval, the workshop that weekend would be canceled, and I'd be asked to board the next plane home.

Even though our prayer ministry teams operated on a well-thought-out set of guidelines, none of it had been put in writing as of that point.

I am forever grateful that this church asked me to articulate the foundational beliefs, guidelines, and values that are key to positioning healing prayer ministry as a vital ministry in the local church.

Here's my original presentation, unchanged ever since.

1. *The ultimate desired outcome for healing prayer is not the healing itself.* Rather, the outcome we ultimately seek is increased intimacy with the Father. *Note*: Every miraculous healing that Jesus did was a temporary solution; however, intimacy with the Father is for eternity. Therefore, if all we are asking for is the healing itself, we are not asking for nearly enough.

   • This posture helps keep us from developing "goofy theology";

   • This posture helps keep us from reducing prayer to formulas or magical thinking; *Note*: Healing prayer is not a panacea[4] nor is it a shortcut to deeper spirituality or maturity; and

   • All people are called to pray for healing but not all people will necessarily be gifted.

2. *Healing prayer is positioned in the church as one aspect of the overall spiritual formation process.* It's an important aspect, but only one part of it:

   • Healing prayer ministry must not become the featured ministry of the church (which is better for the long-term sustainability of the ministry);

   • Healing prayer works best and has the potential to have the greatest impact when an environment of safety has been intentionally cultivated by the church's senior leadership throughout every ministry and department in the church;

---

4. I appreciate this statement, which is familiar in a number of books written by Dr. Charles Kraft.

- Be aware: prayer ministries may attract some of the *wrong people*, those who crave attention; and

- A developmental process and mature leadership is required to identify, train, deploy, and shepherd prayer team members.

3. *Creating a safe environment for prayer ministry is essential:*

   - It is important not to "anoint"/elevate people too quickly as team members; so, be known for choosing people carefully and developing them well; and

   - Confidentiality is a primary concern of prayer ministry and for creating a safe environment in the church; it [always] starts at the top!

4. *Common Myths:*

   - *Everything is spiritual warfare:* the enemy gets way too much credit; we lose sight of personal responsibility; and

   - *Nothing is spiritual warfare:* ignorance leads to unnecessary defeats and casualties; we fail to use the spiritual authority that God intended us to use.

5. *Other Considerations:*

   - Only God does the healing, but he likes to work in partnership with his people; *Note:* That's why we call the healing prayer ministry at the church where I serve, *Sola Dei* (Latin for "only God");

   - How we view spiritual gifts, especially when we're discussing gifts pertaining to the miraculous, are important conversations to have; and

   - All of the spiritual gifts follow the same rules.

   Notes:

   - Things *do not* have to get messy because you have opened the door to the Holy Spirit!

- We need to know that no matter how profoundly a person is gifted, it is not an indication of spirituality or maturity.

HEALING PRAYER SPECIALTIES

I have met many people over the years who have prayed for a person to be physically healed but saw no apparent results, leading them to conclude that they had absolutely no gifting to be used by the Lord to see people get healed.

For anyone who has prayed without result and concluded the same, it would be helpful to take into account that there are various types of "healing prayer specialties."

Some people seem to be particularly gifted to pray for healing of specific illnesses and see more favorable results when doing so. What biblical evidence might there be to explain why this is?

Dr. Charles Kraft talked about three of the spiritual gifts listed in 1 Corinthians 12 as being gifts of *double plurality*, meaning that, in the original language, both of the operative words are written in plural; for example, the *gifts of healings*.[5]

So, what does this mean?

It's important to note that we can learn a great deal about how things work in the spiritual realm by looking for clues in the material world. For example, in the medical profession, if someone has a heart condition, what kind of specialist would they go to? A cardiologist, right?

If someone has problems with their feet, they would seek out a podiatrist.

If someone has a toothache, you know they'd head straight for a dentist's office.

All of them are doctors, but each one is armed with a specific medical expertise. Each has an area of specialization. In the same way, there is evidence that people who pray for healing have been given certain specialties to pray for, in which they will see more favorable healing results.

---

5. A concept from Dr. Kraft's lectures and syllabus, Fuller Seminary.

Years ago, I had the opportunity to pray for someone who had been suffering with lower back pain for many years. In fact, she had undergone surgery to insert a metal rod to support her spine. Up until that time, I had seen very little, if any, improvement in those for whom I had prayed for a physical healing.

This time, however, this woman reported that all of her pain had completely vanished as I prayed. Now, whenever I hear that somebody has some sort of back pain, I've made it a point to ask, "May I pray for your back?"[6]

Most of those people have shown improvement: some immediately, some over a period of time.

To this day, I look for backs to pray for and often see positive results. I also see healing and breakthrough regularly when praying for deep level (emotional) healing.

I don't share this to boast. I can't. None of this is based on me. Spiritual gifts are gifts of grace, distributed as the Holy Spirit determines (see 1 Corinthians 12:11).

For this reason, I encourage you to pray for healing even if you don't think that you're gifted to do so. Pray for as many people as you can and pay close attention to the times you notice any improvement—or when a complete healing occurs. I suggest keeping a journal to help you track how you might be gifted to pray.

When prayers are repeatedly answered favorably over a period of time, it may indicate an anointing—a healing prayer specialty!

---

6. It's important to know that I invited three female team members to join me in praying for this woman. I was the only person who prayed out loud, but I'm confident that the divine healing which occurred was aided by the multiplicity of spiritual gifts present in that brief moment of prayer. God was responsible for the healing.

12

Deep-Level Healing

IN SEVERAL OF THE epistles, Paul uses the metaphor of a *race* to describe life in Christ and the believer's formation towards Christlikeness.

To the Church at Corinth, Paul writes,

> Do you not know that in a race all the runners run, but only one gets the prize? Run in such a way as to get the prize. (1 Corinthians 9:24)

Using the same metaphor, I pose the following question:

Have you noticed how some people run the Christian race relatively free from encumbrances, while others run with what appear to be giant ankle weights, making every stride painfully difficult?

I do.

Some people really do carry an extraordinary amount of pain from their past wounds and present circumstances, and actually have a much more difficult time doing life on a daily basis.

But there's good news. It doesn't necessarily need to be this way.

Healing at the deepest levels of our being is possible.

Freedom and wholeness is available in Jesus.

Some of the areas that can be addressed in deep-level healing, which may have been caused by pain and abuse inflicted by others, traumatic life events, or sinful choices we have made in the past, include the following:

- *Identifying and canceling the negative effects of verbal cursing;* "The tongue has the power of life and death, and those who love it will eat its fruit." (Proverbs 18:21)

- *Identifying and canceling the negative effects of self-cursing;* "It is a trap for a man to dedicate something rashly and only later to consider his vows." (Proverbs 20:25)

- *Identifying lies that are believed as true (through inner conversations and scripts) which keeps people from realizing their God-given potential;* "You belong to your father, the devil, and you want to carry out your father's desires. He was a murderer from the beginning, not holding to the truth, for there is no truth in him. When he lies, he speaks his native language, for he is a liar and the father of lies." (John 8:44)

- *Breaking unwholesome soul ties (soul = mind, emotions, will) to those that have been hurtful in the past and that fragment wholeness and complete freedom;* "Until we all reach unity in the faith and in the knowledge of the Son of God and become mature, attaining to the whole measure of the fullness of Christ." (Ephesians 4:13)

- *Breaking intimate bonding (through consensual and non-consensual sex) and addressing any shame that is related to such actions;* "Do you not know that your bodies are members of Christ himself? Shall I then take the members of Christ and unite them with a prostitute? Never! Do you not know that he who unites himself with a prostitute is one with her in body? For it is said, 'The two will become one flesh.'" (1 Corinthians 6:15–16)

- *Healing memories of painful or traumatic events;* Much of our memories are stored as "pictures." *Episodic memory*[1] is the

---

1. Wikipedia has a helpful explanation for understanding more about *episodic memory.*

name given to the capacity to consciously remember personally experienced events and situations. It's one of the major cognitive capacities enabled by the brain.

HOW HEALING OFTEN WORKS

A person's healing process often happens over time, layer by layer.

This means that when a significant breakthrough occurs in someone's life, it's usually followed by a period of time when they learn to live in their newfound healing/freedom.

It may take several months or years for a person to learn how to steward the healing and freedom that they have been given.

I sometimes wonder why it works this way and conclude that God knows exactly how much we can handle at any given time.

After God does his part, he invites us to do our part.

It isn't unusual for the Lord to bring healing and breakthrough as a result of the prayer process. We've seen him heal physical illnesses and emotional brokenness, setting people free from the forces of darkness and affirming that he is the One who heals and brings people into wholeness and fullness of life.

However, it's important to remember that healing prayer does not offer a panacea for every past hurt or relational difficulty.

In fact, healing prayer is only one aspect of the overall spiritual formation and healing process, and it doesn't replace the need to regularly nurture one's spiritual and personal growth through these practices:

- Scripture reading and memorization;

- Consistent personal and corporate worship;

- Regular rhythms of prayer;

- Walking with others in authentic, Christ-centered community; and

- Giving generously of one's self and resources in service to others.

No matter how dramatic the results of healing prayer may be, they don't provide a shortcut to one's continued spiritual growth or emotional maturity.

Everyone who receives prayer should also avail themselves of any needed medical and psychological support, in addition to any treatment recommended by reliable members of the medical community.

CLEANSING/DELIVERANCE PRAYER

This topic is not without some disagreement among followers of Jesus from different faith traditions and theological frameworks.

For the first half of my life, my own faith tradition seemed either to deny the possibility that a Christian could be demonized or to avoid the conversation altogether. To the best of my recollection, it was simply never discussed.

Soon after I was introduced to healing prayer, I witnessed several prayer sessions in which the prayee required "cleansing" prayer that set them free from various forms of demonic attachment. What impressed me most in those early days, as it still continues to do to this day, is what a highly positive difference this specific type of prayer can make in a person's life.

There's also something so wonderfully *Jesus-like* when one has the privilege to participate in leading a person out of spiritual darkness and into the loving arms of our Heavenly Father. Jesus' ministry mandate continues to find expression among his people to this day:

> The Spirit of the Lord is on me, because he has anointed
> me to proclaim good news to the poor. He has sent me to
> proclaim freedom for the prisoners and recovery of sight
> for the blind, to set the oppressed free, to proclaim the
> year of the Lord's favor. (Luke 4:18–19)

There was once a time when many in the Western world believed that demonization only happened elsewhere in the world, particularly in places where various occult practices, shamanism, and the worship of pagan deities were on open display for all to see.

However, there has been a major shift in the US over the last three decades as an increased fascination with the dark side of the spiritual realm has grown prevalent, as reflected in much prime-time television programming. We see a steady increase in programs that feature seemingly benevolent versions of the demonic, the occult, and black magic, their practitioners often portrayed by attractive and heroic-type celebrities who wield tremendous influence on culture.

But it gets worse: several major retailers carry "cute" illustrated children's books that teach kids how to summon demons![2]

Not only does this desensitize people to darkness, it normalizes—even glamorizes—the demonic.

In the original *Star Wars* movie trilogy, there's a sequence in which Luke Skywalker trains rigorously with Master Yoda on the swampy, mist-enshrouded planet of Dagobah. Exhausted, Luke pauses to ask Yoda if the dark side of the Force is stronger than the light side.

Yoda rightly responds that the dark side of the Force is not stronger but is far more *seductive*.

We mustn't be naive on this matter. The dark side of the spiritual realm is very seductive and full of deception. It promises to deliver what the heart longs for, but can only offer a poor, unsustainable counterfeit of the real thing, which can only be found in Christ.

The seductive nature of witchcraft is reflected in the explosive growth of Wicca in the United States. A study by Trinity College in Connecticut reported an estimated eight thousand Wiccans in 1990; by 2008, that number had grown to about three hundred forty thousand.[3]

2. This is no joke and ought to be taken very seriously. I offer the following link to demonstrate the shift that has occurred in recent years to entice children to participate in occult activity. https://vigilantcitizen.com/latestnews/a-childrens-book-of-demons-teaches-children-how-to-summon-demons/

3. Singh-Kurz, S. & Kopf, D. (2018, October 4). *The US witch population has seen an astronomical rise.* Retrieved from https://qz.com/quartzy/1411909/the-explosive-growth-of-witches-wiccans-and-pagans-in-the-us/

Startling statistics such as this provide a clarion call for local churches to be adequately prepared to serve those who'll need deliverance prayer ministry to help them break free from deception and darkness—and find their true heart's desires in Jesus Christ.

HOW DOES AN INDIVIDUAL BECOME DEMONIZED?

A person could be demonized or oppressed when demons have an "entry point" or an "open door" to gain access into his or her life.

An individual may invite demonization by overtly pursuing occult power and participating in various occult practices listed here:[4]

- Occult literature,

- Witchcraft,

- Black magic or white magic,

- Satanism,

- Spiritualism,

- Victim of abuse,

- Hallucinogenic drugs, and

- Choosing to live with anger, bitterness, resentment.

Demons may also gain an entry point into one's life through the actions of another, especially if that person is an authority figure in his or her life (e.g., a parent) and has opened a door to the spiritual realm. In such cases, the person's involvement is passive, yet he or she remains vulnerable because of the actions of an authority figure over him or her.

Some of these actions may include the following:

- Dedication of children to various deities (often done in temples);

---

4. I would like to mention that this is *not* an exhaustive list but rather a representative list of possibilities that could lead to demonization.

- Involvement with shamans and following their direction for prosperity, good luck, etc.;

- Generational sin patterns/spirits (also called *familiar spirits*);

- Evoking demons through practices of necromancy, seances, etc.; and

- Various occult practices.

When we address the problem of demonization, regardless of who is responsible for opening the door to the dark side of the spiritual realm, we must also take into account the specific *legal rights* the enemy may have to demonize a person.

Basic steps for canceling the legal rights of the enemy and closing doors to demonization may include these:

- Renouncing occult practices (the specific actions of others or your own actions);

- Forgiving those responsible for opening spiritual doors to the spiritual realm;

- Asking God for forgiveness and repenting of your own actions;

- Commanding the demons to leave; sending them to wherever Jesus requires them to go; and

- Destroying any occult objects or reading materials that may have been introduced into a person's life and living space.

Note: It is strongly recommended that the above steps for cleansing prayer (also known as deliverance prayer) be done with the guidance of a prayer minister who is trained and experienced in deliverance prayer.

THE HEALING PRAYER TEAM

The name of the healing prayer team that I've served for the past fifteen years is called *Sola Dei*. It's based on the Latin phrase for "only God," reminding every team member that only God does the healing. We don't.

It's a very important thing to remind ourselves. It cultivates both gratitude and humility.

Potential team members begin their training with sixteen hours of interactive lectures and prayer practicums. Team leaders—or *Sola Dei* coaches—often share their own personal journey in healing prayer and how prayer has changed the trajectory of their lives. Team leaders also make themselves available to offer personalized coaching to team members during the prayer practicums.

Our curriculum focuses on the three levels of healing prayer: physical, or surface level prayer; emotional, or deep-level prayer; and spiritual, or deliverance prayer. Every team member must have a comprehensive understanding of how each level interrelates and overlaps with the others.

Following this training, those who express an interest in being part of the *Sola Dei* team meet with our point person for an informal interview, which helps to discern the candidate's suitability for this ministry. Those who are invited to join the team begin an apprenticeship for a period of no less than six months.

A mandatory part of this apprenticeship is for team members to receive their own healing prayer appointments with other *Sola Dei* team members. The reason for this? You've probably heard that "hurt people hurt people." Those who haven't been healed of their own pain risk inflicting pain on others.

SOLA DEI HEALING PRAYER TEAM VALUES AND GUIDELINES

- *Sola Dei*—only God (heals);
- Intimacy with the Father is the ultimate desired outcome of prayer;
- Confidentiality (Prayees can share if they wish, but team members cannot);
- Clean as you go (team members practice forgiveness/healing in their own lives);

- Serve others from the overflow of a personal, love relationship with Jesus;
- God gets all of the credit;
- We live our lives in community together;
- Mutual submission, mutual accountability; and
- Continually choose to be a nameless and faceless people.

PART FIVE

Intercessory Prayer

13

Cultivating a Culture of Prayer

WHEN IT COMES TO prayer gaining real traction in the church, and for the church to begin to experience the transformative nature of prayer, it all has to start at the top.

Wholehearted commitment by senior leadership to cultivating a *culture of prayer* is a key priority.

When proposing an increased culture of prayer in your ministry context, be sure to communicate the "why" behind it. Leaders need to know the "why" if they are to offer a wholehearted "yes and amen" to this prayer initiative.

In some churches and ministry organizations, this may need to be carefully communicated, with ample time given to influencers to process—after all, such a shift towards prayer can be radical in many people's spiritual worldviews.

However, when this spiritual shift starts at the top, it will eventually saturate the hearts and minds of those who follow, and prayer will become the core value on which all spiritual formation and ministry activities have as a foundation. Not only will prayer have positive impact in the way ministry is done, it will also have an impact on how leaders begin to relate to one another as they seek the face of God together.

Oswald Chambers offers his insight on the primacy of prayer:

Prayer does not equip us for greater works—prayer is the greater work. Yet we think of prayer as some common sense exercise of our higher powers that simply prepares us for God's work. In the teachings of Jesus Christ, prayer is the working of the miracle of redemption in me, which produces the miracle of redemption in others, through the power of God.[1]

WHAT IS INTERCESSORY PRAYER?

Just as there are many types of people with different interests, temperaments, talents, and gifts, there are also several types of prayer, each with their own designated purpose, each one suited to different prayer team members.

One of them is intercessory prayer. What is it, and how does it impact the spiritual realm?

First of all, intercession is not a synonym for all types of prayer.

"Prayer, generally speaking, means talking to God. Intercession is coming to God on behalf of another. All intercession is prayer, but not all prayer is intercession."[2]

The word intercession comes from the Latin *inter*, which means "between," and *cedere*, which means "to go." Thus, whenever you engage in intercessory prayer, you're acting as a *go-between*.[3]

There are things that God desires to do but doesn't *until* a partnership has been formed when we pray, when we seek the heart of God for the things that He has placed on our hearts to pray. This is the way it works in the spiritual realm, a principle that is aptly illustrated in the book of Ezekiel:

> Then the word of the LORD came to me: "Son of man,
> the people of Israel have become dross to me; all of them

---

1. Chambers, *My Utmost for His Highest*, October 17. Retrieved from https://utmost.org/the-key-of-the-greater-work/.

2. Some of my best thinking in this section was influenced by Dr. C. Peter Wagner to whom I owe a debt of gratitude for mentoring me in intercessory prayer through several of his books. In particular, Wagner, *Prayer Shield*, 26.

3. Wagner, *Prayer Shield*, 26.

are the copper, tin, iron and lead left inside a furnace. They are but the dross of silver. . . . I looked for someone among them who would build up the wall and stand before me in the gap on behalf of the land so I would not have to destroy it, but I found no one. So I will pour out my wrath on them and consume them with my fiery anger, bringing down on their own heads all they have done, declares the Sovereign LORD." (Ezekiel 22:17–31)

Could there be a more devastating passage in the Bible that clearly demonstrates the requirement of intercessory prayer for God to act on behalf of those who will pray?

God always does all of his part, but he doesn't do our part.

Agree or disagree?

Intercession, or joining God in the things that are in his heart to do, is our part.

I submit to leadership in the local church that ministry not bathed in intercessory prayer is likely to be lacking in the power of God and in any real and lasting effectiveness.

Keep in mind, however, that intercession isn't about trying to manipulate God.

Intercession is about partnering with God to release into existence what he *already desires* to accomplish. The importance of intercessory prayer to the health, well-being, and effectiveness of the local church *cannot be overstated.*

My understanding of the extreme importance of intercessory prayer began less than ten years ago, when a team from my church was invited to train leaders in three African countries.

A PERSONAL AWAKENING

In March of 2012, I came face-to-face with the extent of my ignorance in regards to intercessory prayer.

I received an email note from Annie, a dear friend who is a vicar with the Church of England, whose ministry focus is ministering to the marginalized and mostly unchurched people of the city.

Annie, who is well-versed in praying for the healing of broken people, asked me if I would bring a team to the Democratic Republic of the Congo (DRC). We were invited to join her in teaching a healing prayer workshop and offer healing prayer appointments to seventy pastors and key leaders on the eastern border of the DRC.

Perhaps you've heard of this war-torn country being referred to as the "heart of darkness" on the African continent. It wasn't long before I learned that 70 percent of the women in DRC have been raped by soldiers as one of the tactics used to terrorize and demoralize a nation into submission.

Just two days after receiving this request, my supervisor forwarded another request from the point leader of an organization called Y-Malawi, which was a collaboration of seven different mission organizations (including World Vision at the time) that partnered together to do holistic community transformation in two large regions of Malawi.

Our church was a participating church that sent short-term teams annually to serve the people under the banner of Y-Malawi. In his email, the point leader stated that he had heard a little about what we were doing with healing prayer ministry, and on that basis, he approached us with this: "For the upcoming year, Y-Malawi has declared war on malaria and on witchcraft. So, would it be possible for you to come to Malawi and help us understand further what it means to have declared war on witchcraft?"

Could these two requests, within forty-eight hours of each other, simply be a coincidence?

It didn't feel like it was. I knew that I had to take these opportunities to the Lord in prayer.

The magnitude of each request quickly put me in touch with some of my insecurities as I realized that I would be in way over my head.

My many years of helping people get free from demonic oppression and demonization didn't mean I was qualified to teach leaders in Malawi how to combat witchcraft, which was commonly practiced in many of the villages that we would be visiting.

Could I learn enough in time and prepare a team for such an ambitious assignment? Was it hubris on my part for even considering the possibility?

When I sensed a "green light" to put together a team to serve leaders in both of these places, I became a voracious reader on the subject of high-level spiritual warfare—a topic inseparable from intercessory prayer.

The more I learned about intercession, the more I realized that I had been neglecting the most important and foundational kind of prayer that is the basis for every ministry of the church.

I clearly remember a day when, while studying and feeling remorse for my ignorance, I prayed, "Lord, I'm so sorry, I didn't know."

"It's okay, Ed," the Holy Spirit gently and kindly impressed upon my heart, "but now, it's time."

In October of 2012, our prayer team from Southern California joined the London team to begin the first of two assignments in Africa. Did I mention that I was very selective to invite the most experienced and mature prayer team members whom I believed would be up for a challenging travel schedule and intense ministry demands?

Before unpacking some of the key features of intercessory prayer and offering recommendations for intentionally mobilizing intercession in the local church, I want to share a story from the Malawi leg of our trip.

After a solid week of training and many individual prayer appointments for the seventy leaders who attended the workshop in the DRC, we said goodbye to the London team whom we had grown to love in a very short time and boarded a red-eye flight to Malawi.

By the time we landed, the team was physically exhausted and emotionally spent.

Our host in Malawi was expecting us to be ready to hit the ground running, which was what I was thinking as well. It soon became apparent that it would have been wise to build a full-day break between the two assignments, but I hadn't considered that when planning the itinerary. I really should have known better, being all-too-familiar with the rigors of international travel and ministry.

I had unwittingly set up a perfect storm and was caught completely off guard by it.

Our first full day in Malawi was extremely challenging. The team dragged themselves through the day, completely exhausted. Morale sank low. The energy and vigor of the previous week had evaporated. As for me, every button to my fears and insecurities was being pushed.

I started to believe that I was the worst leader ever.

I began to question every decision I had made in the planning of this trip.

I concluded that I was a miserable failure, losing any hope of salvaging the remaining part of the trip.

When I woke up the next day, I sensed that mutiny was about to ensue. In desperation, I prayed out loud—actually, I looked up and shouted, "Lord, wake up the intercessors!" (It was daytime in Malawi but late at night in California.)

If anything was going to improve, it wasn't going to happen because of my poor leadership. It would have to be by the hand of God.

About an hour later, as we were preparing to board the bus and travel to various villages for an entire day of "prayer mapping,"[4] or interviewing village leaders to help develop a comprehensive prayer strategy for the region, I "felt" an inner voice—a faint impression that I call the inner, inaudible voice of God.

Just two words were impressed on me: *hovering spirit.*

Hovering what?

I didn't know what a hovering spirit was. I'd never heard of such a thing. But I had nothing to lose, so I called the team into an awkward huddle in the cramped aisle of the bus.

I told them that I needed to pray a brief prayer for them. In a most awkward fashion, I stretched my arms over the team and prayed these words, "In Jesus' name, I take authority over the hovering spirit that is over this team and I cancel all your works and

---

4. Otis, Jr., *Informed Intercession*, 77–97.

assignments against us. I command you to leave us now. Go to the place Jesus tells you to go. Do not return; do not send any others. In Jesus' name."

Afterwards, everyone quietly returned to their seats.

No one said a word. There was no indication that the prayer had any impact whatsoever.

Until a few minutes later.

For the first time in two days, I started hearing some light-hearted banter. Then, I saw some smiles breaking and even heard some laughter.

The team was back in true form. We had a breakthrough.

Upon our return to the US, I checked in with some of the intercessors who were praying for our team and asked if they noticed any unusual occurrences. Two of the intercessors told me that they "were awakened" one of the evenings (yes, it was around the same time that I had shouted out to the Lord) and felt that the team was in some sort of trouble and needed immediate prayer.

Without a doubt, breakthrough occurred because the intercessors prayed for our team.

I don't know how I could have been so ignorant for so long. How could I not know that intercessory prayer is foundational to ministry effectiveness and that to serve God in any significant way without intercession is dangerous?

I will always be grateful for the two invitations that required much intensive study and team preparation. They would prove to be invaluable in my continuing education and growing understanding of the power of God, which can only be fully released through the act of intercessory prayer. To this day, I'm convinced that my own prayer effectiveness would be minimal at best if not for the opportunity I was given to be totally in over my head!

For the balance of this chapter, I'll share some of my thoughts about how to begin identifying, developing, mobilizing, and shepherding prayer intercessors.

IDENTIFYING INTERCESSORS

This just might be one of the most important and strategic things that senior leadership can do to further the mission of the local church.

Those who'll do the work to identify, cultivate, mobilize, and shepherd intercessors to pray for the church and its leadership will begin to notice an increase in each of these significant areas:

- Tenderized hearts of people for the desires that God has for his children;

- A deepening reliance and trust in God's provision to accomplish his purposes in the Church; and

- The power of God more noticeable in daily ministry effectiveness.

But truth be told, identifying genuine intercessors is more easily said than done. The reasons for this are threefold:

- The temperament of most intercessors gravitates towards introversion; intercessors are often content to remain unnoticed and tend to fly under the radar of church leadership;

- The nature of an intercessor's ministry pretty much keeps them in solitude; intercessors do their best work in "prayer closets"; and

- There seems to be consensus among those who live in the world of prayer people that only about 5 percent of the people in the church have been given this rather unique assignment—to pray in a way that has a gifted quality and in which the person feels called to it.

You know you're an intercessor if you have these tendancies:

- You love, love, love to pray;

- You're awake most mornings between four and five o'clock and are compelled to pray;

- You only have twenty minutes to pray, but by the time you leave your prayer closet you realize that nearly two hours have gone by; and

- You live to be in the presence of your Father in heaven and intimacy with him is the only reward that you seek.

I once read this list to a gathering of nearly forty people. When I was done, at least five people in the room were in tears. It was a holy moment in which some real-deal intercessors felt understood and validated—maybe for the first time ever—for their hard work and the sacrifice required to intercede for whatever God puts on their hearts to pray for.

Identifying intercessors is not easy and will require your prayerful vigilance and patient intentionality.

Here's the good news: you don't need very many to form a spiritually powerful team. Be sure to focus on quality, with genuinely gifted individuals, over quantity.

DEVELOPING INTERCESSORS

Once you've identified those whom you wish to invite to be part of a team (I suggest that this team, along with all other prayer teams, be recruited *by invitation only*), meet with them for a one-on-one visit over coffee or perhaps at the church office.

Use the time to share your vision: to cultivate a culture of prayer in the church, to be led by the Holy Spirit, etc. You might want to create an outline for how the team will function, what the commitment will entail, and what the guidelines for the team will be. This could be especially important to determine *ahead of time*. Every prayer team person needs to know and align with the vision, ethos, and theological posture of the church as well.

Finally, invite the potential prayer team member to pray about your request, and ask them to only accept your invitation if they have a strong leading that this *an assignment* from the Lord for this particular season.

This is the type of person you want as a team member, as opposed to someone who simply says "yes" to please you or to fill a void in his or her own life.

I'll often give a potential leader a book (in this case, a book on intercessory prayer that closely reflects your church's theological posture) and ask them to meet with me again after they've read it so that you can discuss the book together.

MOBILIZING INTERCESSORS

Once you've assembled your team of intercessors, invite them to come together for an initial kick-off gathering, perhaps over a meal. Let everyone get acquainted as you break bread together. After dinner, go over the same topics that you discussed individually and reiterate the time commitment, expectations, future team gathering schedule, and any other pertinent information.

Group meetings should probably happen at least twice per year. In some cases, monthly meetings might be optimum for building community, doing corporate development, and praying together.

Keep in mind that intercessors in particular do not need (or necessarily want) a lot of group time together to do their ministry of intercession for the church and its leaders. I would strongly suggest, however, that you give the intercessors access to one point person such as a staff pastor to connect with when they feel a need to discuss what they're discerning in prayer.

SHEPHERDING INTERCESSORS

Generally speaking, I have found that intercessors tend to be very low maintenance. However, a friend of mine once reminded me, "Ed, just because someone is *low* maintenance doesn't mean that they're *no* maintenance."

Point well taken.

Intercessors need to be both acknowledged and appreciated.

Acknowledge intercessors for the very important role they have in the church. The ministry that they do for others provides much of the fuel for the many other ministries that are happening.

Appreciate intercessors because intercession comes at a cost. The life of an intercessor probably means early to bed and early to rise, to begin praying for those who will still get to sleep for another two or three more hours. Intercessory prayer is hard work that requires commitment and sacrifice. So, remember to tell the intercessors under your care, "Thank you for what you do. Your intercession matters more than either of us will ever know this side of eternity."

I never intend to suggest that any one type of prayer ministry is more important than another. I'm definitely not qualified to do that. Over the years I've gained a special love for every type of prayer ministry that I've participated in. What I do know for sure is that we cannot survive, in any meaningful way, without the ministry of intercession.

The Church needs to acknowledge this vital ministry and the people who obediently respond to this particular God-given assignment.

PART SIX

Prayers for the Church

IN THIS SECTION, I'D like to offer a kind of prayer "tool box"—
several important types of prayer that can be employed as a regular
part of one's life and in any ministry context.

14

Consecration Prayer

CONSECRATION IS THE ACT of dedicating to God whatever is in need of his grace. This is done deliberately and intentionally to bring those things under the rule and authority of Jesus.

Consecration is the essential first step of every believer for God's provision and protection to flow in his or her life.

As John Eldredge writes, "Consecration is usually the first act of effective prayer; until this occurs it is hard to see anything else good happen. . . . Consecration is healing the 'connection,' so that God's power can flow into our bodies."[1]

EXAMPLES OF WHAT TO CONSECRATE

- Consecrate yourself (your body, mind, emotions, words, spiritual gifts, anointing, etc.) at the beginning of each day;

- Consecrate your home *before* you begin to cleanse it or bless it;

- Consecrate a relationship; and

- Consecrate your work.

1. Eldredge, *Moving Mountains*, 100–101.

Note: When we do the work of God expressly, we place ourselves in a collision of two kingdoms. It takes intentionality to bring things under and into the Kingdom of God.[2]

The sixth chapter of Isaiah gives us an example of the need to be consecrated *before the Lord.*

> "Woe to me!" I cried. "I am ruined! For I am a man of unclean lips, and I live among a people of unclean lips, and my eyes have seen the King, the Lord Almighty."
>
> Then one of the seraphim flew to me with a live coal in his hand, which he had taken with tongs from the altar. With it he touched my mouth and said, "See, this has touched your lips; your guilt is taken away and your sin atoned for." (Isaiah 6:5–7)

ANTICIPATING A QUESTION

Someone may say, "As a Christian, I am already cleansed and declared righteous on the basis of Christ's death on the cross."

This statement is absolutely true regarding our *position in Christ.*

However, *practically* speaking, there is much biblical evidence to support the need for us to participate in our own re-alignment (an aspect of our sanctification process) before the Lord.

In John 15:4–11, Jesus tells us to remain (or abide) in him, implying that we are apt to wander away from him. Jesus also reminds us that apart from him we can do nothing (see v. 5).

In Colossians 2:18–19, The Apostle Paul is writing to those who have somehow lost connection with Jesus by various means. It is important to note that we have an enemy who constantly desires to separate us from God and thereby neutralize our effectiveness in the work of his Kingdom.

---

2. For a broader study on consecration see Eldredge, "Consecration— Bringing things under the rule of Jesus," *Moving Mountains.*

ANALOGY OF CONSECRATION

Think about going to hear a world-class orchestra play a magnificent piece of music.

The first thing that you'd notice is that each of the professional musicians will prepare themselves even before the conductor comes out onto the stage.

You see and hear each one tune their instruments, beginning with the instruments that play softer.

Only after all of the instruments are in tune does the conductor step out onto the stage.

What do you think you might have heard if the musicians hadn't prepared beforehand?

Consecration prayer is prayer to prepare ourselves to be in tune with God, the master conductor.

OLD TESTAMENT EXAMPLES OF CONSECRATION

For the priests who brought the sacrifices before the Lord on behalf of the people, ceremonial purification represented the inward purification in which they were to live before the Lord.

> Moses, Aaron and the whole Israelite community did with the Levites just as the Lord commanded Moses. The Levites purified themselves and washed their clothes. Then Aaron presented them as a wave offering before the Lord and made atonement for them to purify them. After that, the Levites came to do their work at the tent of meeting under the supervision of Aaron and his sons. They did with the Levites just as the Lord commanded Moses. (Numbers 8:20–22)

> The Lord said to Moses, "I am going to come to you in a dense cloud, so that the people will hear me speaking with you and will always put their trust in you." Then Moses told the Lord what the people had said. And the Lord said to Moses, "Go to the people and consecrate them today and tomorrow. Have them wash their clothes and be ready by the third day, because on that day the

Lord will come down on Mount Sinai in the sight of all the people." (Exodus 19:9–11)

Joshua told the people, "Consecrate yourselves, for tomorrow the Lord will do amazing things among you." (Joshua 3:5)

NEW TESTAMENT PERSPECTIVE OF CONSECRATION

Consecration as revealed in the New Testament is for every believer in Christ. It's the basis for every spiritual experience.

Consecration is the giving of ourselves to the Lord to become "a living sacrifice." Paul writes:

> Therefore, I urge you, brothers and sisters, in view of God's mercy, to offer your bodies as a living sacrifice, holy and pleasing to God—this is your true and proper worship. (Romans 12:1)

In the Old Testament, a sacrifice was something set apart for God by being put on the altar. When people offered it to God, it no longer belonged to the one offering it. It belonged to God, for his use and his satisfaction.

When we consecrate ourselves to the Lord, we ourselves become a *living sacrifice.*

We completely surrender the claims/rights we have on ourselves and willingly place all that we are under the rule and authority of Jesus Christ for his use and for his glory.

In this New Testament analogy, the follower of Christ is simultaneously the temple of the Lord, the sacrifice, and a member of the royal priesthood which administers the sacrifice on behalf of the people.

> You also, like living stones, are being built into a spiritual house to be a holy priesthood, offering spiritual sacrifices acceptable to God through Jesus Christ. . . . But you are a chosen people, a royal priesthood, a holy nation, God's special possession, that you may declare the praises of him

who called you out of darkness into his wonderful light.
(1 Peter 2:5, 9)

SAMPLE: DAILY PRAYER OF CONSECRATION

In the name of the Lord Jesus Christ, I bring all that I am to my Heavenly Father as a living sacrifice which is my true and proper act of worship. I present my body, my mind, and my emotions, along with each of my abilities, talents, and spiritual gifts to you, Lord Jesus, and bring them under Your reign and rule. May I be used by You as an instrument of Your grace, mercy, and righteousness.

I ask for the blood of my Lord Jesus to cleanse me and for the fire of the Holy Spirit to purge me of anything that would hinder my love relationship with You, Lord Jesus. I present myself to be used for Your purposes and that Your will be done on earth as it is in heaven. Holy Spirit, come and fill me to overflowing; I present myself to You and place myself under Your complete dominion.

Today, I make the declaration that I belong to You, Heavenly Father. I have been purchased with the shed blood of Jesus, so I belong only to You. I dedicate myself to You once again. I present all that I am as a vessel for Your power and glory to be known. My desire is to be used to accomplish Your purposes under Your watchful care and protection throughout this day. In Jesus' name, I pray. Amen.

15

Commissioning and Impartation Prayers

THERE ARE TWO TYPES of prayer that are essentially *prayers of agreement:* prayers in which we have an opportunity to come into agreement with what we see God *already doing* in the lives of people and then to stand in agreement with him.

The first is *commissioning prayer,* which I think of as a corporate blessing for either an individual or a group that is about to *do something* such as a new ministry assignment or ministry role. This seems to be precisely what the Apostle Paul had in mind for young Timothy at the onset of his public ministry:

> Do not neglect your gift, which was given you through prophecy when the body of elders laid their hands on you. (1 Timothy 4:14)

> For this reason I remind you to fan into flame the gift of God, which is in you through the laying on of my hands. (2 Timothy 1:6)

There is much spiritual power in a corporate prayer setting, especially when there is agreement to release blessing to others who are in transition into the next thing that God calls them to do.

There's also something very empowering to people when the church cultivates a culture in which God's calling of lay leaders is publicly recognized and highlighted by pastors and key leaders of the church. Being attentive to such opportunities to lend their leadership for this purpose is worthwhile, indeed.

The Apostle Paul does offer a word of caution regarding public acknowledgment and the laying of hands on an individual prematurely:

> Do not be hasty in the laying on of hands, and do not share in the sins of others. Keep yourself pure. (1 Timothy 5:22)

IMPARTATION PRAYER

The second is called *impartation prayer,* which is used with an individual when they are about to *receive* something. This is an important type of prayer for when we're coming into agreement with God for something that he has *already given* to someone but has not yet activated within that person.

> For I long to see you so that I may impart to you some spiritual gift to make you strong—that is, that you and I may be mutually encouraged by each other's faith. (Romans 1:11–12)

Impartation of spiritual gifts by another person can be a controversial subject depending on one's traditions and theological biases. I believe that it's important to be as unambiguous as possible about how I see this type of prayer working:

- If God wishes to give a spiritual gift to someone whom you minister to, he may use you in the process to call forth the gift that he is giving to a person;

- It is God himself who determines the spiritual gift, not the person who imparts the gift nor the one who receives it;

All these are the work of one and the same Spirit, and
he distributes them to each one, just as he determines.
(1 Corinthians 12:11)

- An impartation may come from a person who either has or
doesn't have that gift—*they* aren't the source of the gift, after
all; the key is that they act in obedience and impart as God
directs them to do; and

- Impartation can also be given for something other than spiritual gifts, such as an anointing or ability to use a skill or talent
more effectively for Kingdom purposes.

16

Prayer for Home Cleansing and Blessing

HAVE YOU EVER BEEN somewhere and felt that something was *off* about the place?

Has a certain space ever made you feel uneasy and want to leave as soon as possible?

The more attuned you are to the spiritual atmosphere around you, the more you'll be aware that there are definitely places that require spiritual cleansing. If that place is a part of your domain, such as your home or office, you have the authority to cleanse the spiritual atmosphere and get rid of anything that you want out of there.

A "BEAR" VISITS IN THE NIGHT

Early in my tenure as a pastor where I currently serve, I received a request to come to the home of some new friends, "Robert and Irene," a young married couple who were living in a beautiful home in a fairly new housing development.

The couple told me that their young daughter, who was just over a year old, was waking up most nights after midnight, screaming, "Go away bear, go away!"

The startled parents would rush into their daughter's bedroom to comfort her, and every time they did, she would point toward the hallway and tell them with her toddler vocabulary that she had seen a bear.

Irene reported that when she would walk down that same hallway, she'd sometimes get goosebumps. She also said that when her mother would come and stay for a visit, she would refuse to go upstairs because she sensed an evil presence on the second floor.

Three generations of females in the family were attuned to the spiritual atmosphere, and it wasn't good. Robert remained largely unaware that there was a problem. (Not everybody has the same heightened sensitivity to the unseen realm.)

I had invited several members of the prayer team to come with me to the house on a Sunday afternoon, in response to the request for prayer. Upon hearing Robert and Irene's story, we shared with them that they had all of the authority that they needed to cleanse their home of unwanted spiritual "visitors."

Without using spooky language, we coached the couple to appropriate their authority to pray a spiritual cleansing over their entire home, upstairs and downstairs.

When the prayer time was over, we reconvened in the family room to pray blessings for the family. We then said our goodbyes to our grateful friends.

The prayers worked. Robert and Irene later shared that their daughter has slept peacefully at night from that moment on.

WHEN YOU'RE NOT IN KANSAS ANYMORE

I encourage you to pray a cleansing prayer for any space that could be considered your domain, even those that are only temporarily under your authority, for instance, when staying in a hotel room or a guest room when visiting family or friends. These examples are your domain for the duration of your stay.

My church started seeing some breakthrough for short-term mission team members when we started coaching them how to cleanse their sleeping spaces. Returning mission team members reported that cleansing prayer had virtually eliminated incidents of retaliation from nighttime spiritual visitors.

SAMPLE: PRAYER FOR CLEANSING AND BLESSING YOUR HOME (DOMAIN)

[Leader prays aloud with family members present]

In Jesus' name, I consecrate this home to our Father in heaven and declare it to be his domain and under his authority and watchful care.

In Jesus' name, I announce (in agreement with others present) that this prayer of dedication and blessing of our home is done in the authority of *the Lord Jesus Christ of Nazareth who came in the flesh and by the power of his cross, shed blood, resurrection and ascension.*

Heavenly Father, give us Your heart and mind for this time of prayer; release revelation to us as we listen and pray to You. Lord Jesus, please dispatch your heavenly angels to be present and to do as You would instruct them on our behalf. We pause now to dedicate ourselves to You to accomplish Your plans and purposes for our lives. Together, we announce our desire that *"as for me and my household, we will serve the Lord."* (Joshua 24:15)

In Jesus' name, I take full authority over this home to the extreme edges of the property, above, below, and around the entire perimeter.

I take authority over all of the spiritual forces and creatures of evil in the terrestrial realm that have any legal right over this home. I take authority over every lien that the enemy may have attached to our home. I renounce and cancel all claims, liens, past dedications, alliances, and rights that the enemy has on this home and property in the past.

In Jesus' name, I cleanse this entire home and property with the shed blood of the Lord Jesus Christ and with the fire of the Holy Spirit.

In the name of the Lord Jesus Christ of Nazareth, I command that all enemy presence and anything that is not of the Lord Jesus to go immediately to the feet of Jesus at his cross.

In Jesus' name, I forbid any retaliation against me or members of my family who reside in this space (mention each by name). I forbid retaliation or assignments of evil against any of our material possessions or anything else that we hold dear.

In the name and authority of the Lord Jesus Christ, I bless each of my children and family members living in this home, including myself, with the peace of God that passes all understanding. With Your help and grace, Heavenly Father, may we fully appropriate and experience Your love, mercy, grace, power, and favor in each of our lives.

Together, we bless and dedicate ourselves, our home, our material possessions, and all that we hold dear to be Yours and used by You, Heavenly Father, to accomplish Your will on earth as it is in heaven to the glory of the Lord Jesus Christ. In Jesus' name, we pray. Amen.

17

Leading a Twenty-four Hour Silence and Solitude Retreat

THERE IS A PRAYER experience that can be very impactful, even life changing, that does not involve extensive training or a commitment to participate in a prayer team: A twenty-four hour, guided silence and solitude retreat. Over the years, I've established a regular rhythm of leading two silence and solitude retreats per year.

Twenty years ago, I went on my first silence and solitude retreat with the entire staff of the church where I was serving at the time. The church had been given a generous donation to start a small-group-based recovery ministry and had just hired a pastor to lead this pioneering work.

After the foundation for this new ministry had been laid, the recovery pastor invited Brennan Manning to guest preach at our church's weekend worship services and to lead a three-day silence and solitude retreat with the staff at a beautiful Franciscan retreat center in Malibu, California.

The late Brennan Manning was, at one time, a Roman Catholic priest who left the priesthood and got married. He was also a recovering alcoholic. A prolific communicator and author, Brennan's message and poignant stories focused on our God *who loves us just the way we are*, which resonated with countless Christ-followers everywhere. He gained celebrity status in many Protestant circles in the early days of the recovery ministry movement.

I had read about the discipline of silence and solitude in Richard Foster's classic work, *Celebration of Disciplines*,[1] but didn't know anyone who was doing it. So, three full days of silence and solitude with Brennan Manning? Talk about being thrown into the deep end of the pool. But surprisingly, after practicing this ancient spiritual discipline of the Church and connecting with God in the most marvelous way, I knew that a regular rhythm of silence and solitude would be an integral part of my life moving forward.

Introducing others to this discipline, especially ministry leaders and colleagues, has been one of the most rewarding experiences of my life.

GUIDING A TWENTY-FOUR HOUR SILENCE AND SOLITUDE RETREAT

Many of the people who have never done silence and solitude before are understandably nervous the first time they consider going.

Their first question is often, "What am I going to do with all that time?"

This question reflects the average lifestyle of almost everyone I know, including myself: a routine defined by whirlwinds of constant activity with few, if any, moments of extended time of quiet and stillness with God.

To those potential first-timers who are on the fence, I answer this question with a big promise, "If you come, God will meet you there."

And yes, he always does.

I've never received formal training on how to lead a guided silence and solitude retreat. I did, however, pay close attention to Brennan Manning, a former Franciscan priest and retreat master who had a unique understanding of the love of God for his children.

I observed and learned from the best. Here are some key points to facilitate the experience for others.

---

1. Foster, *Celebration of Disciplines*, 96–109.

Location. Preferably, find a place where the beauty of God's creation can be enjoyed. My favorite place to take a group is a Benedictine monastery located in the high desert, a ninety-minute drive from where most people in my church community live. The grounds provide adequate space for walking around and taking short hikes, ideal for those who encounter God more readily while enjoying nature.

Accommodations. We make arrangements with the monastery for each person to have his or her own room, which enhances the experience for every participant and makes it easier to maintain silence for the duration. This monastery has eighteen rooms—a good size for a retreat of this type.

Target audience. After securing dates with the monastery, once in the spring and perhaps again in the fall, get the word out to as many leaders in the church community as possible and give them the opportunity to register before releasing word to the community at large. One of my leadership development goals is to promote a culture in which leaders serve out of an *overflow* of their love relationship with Jesus. Over the years, I've found that silence and solitude retreats are an effective spiritual discipline that serves to cultivate this stated goal.

Guided retreat. I let everyone know ahead of time that once we arrive at the monastery, I would help them think through structuring their time with the Lord. I lead a briefing that includes a question and answer segment, so they are not left to figure out what to do all by themselves.

BRIEFING TOPICS FOR GUIDED RETREATS

- *Freedom to choose.* Participants have total freedom to do what they would like to do. They may rest or take a nap, guilt-free, if they choose. They may come to the meals if they wish to eat in silence with the group or not to eat at all if they prefer.

- *Exploring the grounds.* I suggest areas where participants may explore the grounds.

- *Sharing time.* There is a specific time to come for sharing, which is after breakfast the next morning, when silence is broken together.

- *Intentionality.* Participants are reminded to avoid reading materials, which fill the mind with many thoughts. Instead, they are encouraged to create space to listen, see, and feel the presence of God, and receive from him what he is revealing to them.

- *Worship and prayer.* Participants may worship God and pray to him aloud, if they wish.

- *Monastic tradition.* I share what I've learned about monastic life from the monks. (Protestants tend to be curious about this lifestyle.)

- *Community.* Eating together in silence and observing the community that the monks share at the monastery is always a special experience.

- *Stories.* I share personal stories of what I've experienced and learned since incorporating this spiritual discipline in my own life. I find that a few of these stories encourage most people and prepare them for their own time in silence and solitude.

THE EXPERIENCE

I used to say that if someone creates space to be with God, that he would certainly reveal himself to them. Now I say it differently: if someone creates space for God, they'll hear, see, or feel what he has *already* been revealing to them.

With a little intentionality and practice, we can grow in our ability to connect with God wherever we may be.

My favorite part of the retreat comes at the end when we break our silence with a worship song followed by an hour-and-a-half or so when participants share how they met God in their solitude.

Every story shared is stunningly beautiful and touching. Don't forget to pack some tissue.

PART SEVEN

Principles of Prayer

In this section, I have included two foundation principles that can make a big difference in increasing our effectiveness in prayer. Please pay special attention to avoid *presumptuous prayer* which concludes this chapter.

18

Willingness and Readiness, Prayer of Agreement, Presumptuous Prayer

WILLINGNESS AND READINESS

OFTEN, AN IMPORTANT CRITERION for prayer to be effective is a person's own willingness and readiness, particularly when praying for one's own healing.

Two of my favorite Bible stories of divine healing demonstrate why a person's willingness and readiness are necessary aspects for healing to occur.

In 2 Kings 5:1–19, we're introduced to Naaman, the commander of the army of Aram.

Naaman is a great man of war, highly favored by his king. He contracts leprosy, so the king of Aram sends Naaman south to neighboring Israel and eventually to the home of the prophet Elisha, to be healed by the Lord.

Elisha won't come to the door to greet Naaman, but instead sends his servant with instructions for Naaman to wash himself in the Jordan River. Naaman is insulted but ultimately obeys, is healed, and decides to follow God.

In several ways, Naaman demonstrated his willingness and readiness to be healed:

- Naaman had to overcome his rage after being intentionally insulted by Elisha not greeting him personally;

- Naaman chose to humble himself by washing in a river he thought to be inferior to those in his homeland; and

- After being healed from his leprosy, Naaman returned to Elisha's home to announce that he would be a follower of the Lord, the God of Israel.

The second story is found in the New Testament. It's the account of the woman who had been bleeding for twelve years. Her story is found in Mark 5:24–34. She had suffered under the care of many physicians and had expired all of her resources in hopes of being healed.

- When she learned that Jesus was nearby, she left her home in the hope that she might see him and receive healing;

- Considered ceremonially unclean, the woman had to break many religious rules: she came out into the public and touched many people in the crowd, including a rabbi; and

- Desperation and faith are not the same thing, but when a person is ready to be healed, they may look identical.

The second greatest gift that we have been given by God is our free will. (In case you're wondering, the greatest gift of all is Jesus!)

Along with our free will comes the choice to love and serve him, or to hate and reject him. The choice is ours to make.

God *always* respects our free will. He'll never override a person's free will, not even in favor of his own.

On many occasions, I have seen unwilling people come for physical and deep-level healing prayer in order to placate a loved one that insists that prayer is what is needed. Not once do I recall seeing any improvement in a person's condition when they didn't want to be there.

A person's willingness and readiness are essential. It's an indication of their faith.

THE PRAYER OF AGREEMENT

As discussed earlier, the people of God capture his heart's desire when we make the effort to work together from a genuine posture of interdependence. This principle is reinforced by Jesus in Matthew 18, when he quotes Mosaic law in order to give his hearers insight into how it works in the spiritual realm, regarding praying in agreement with one another. First, take a look at Deuteronomy 19, in which Moses gives instructions for how to make a matter stand up in civil court:

> One witness is not enough to convict anyone accused of any crime or offense they may have committed. A matter must be established by the testimony of two or three witnesses. (Deuteronomy 19:15)

Jesus picks up on what his hearers already know to be true in the natural realm to teach that there is added spiritual authority in the unseen realm when witnesses come together in prayer *in agreement*. The transcendent nature of what Jesus teaches his disciples is revealed in the promise that he will be uniquely present when they establish agreement.

> But if they will not listen, take one or two others along, so that "every matter may be established by the testimony of two or three witnesses." For where two or three gather in my name, there am I with them. (Matthew 18:16, 20)

So, what does it mean to be in agreement? Is Jesus offering his followers a formula that makes God obligated to do whatever is requested if done in a group?

No. Not at all.

In my reasoning, the prayer of agreement is a vigilant, coordinated effort on the part of people who faithfully pray, seek the face of God, and do the necessary work of discernment with church leadership to see if there is corporate agreement for what God desires to do.

At no time in this process can any single person claim special insight or revelation on matters that concern the corporate body of Christ.

PRESUMPTUOUS PRAYER

Doing spiritual warfare wisely is the key to avoiding deadly battle grounds in which believers in Christ become the casualties of spiritual warfare.

Presumptuous prayer[1] occurs when an individual or group of people engage Satan himself and/or other high-ranking spirits, with a view to rebuke or bind them. The Bible identifies these as *rulers* (or *principalities* in some Bible translations), *powers, and world forces.* Notice in this passage:

> For our struggle is not against flesh and blood, but against
> the rulers, against the authorities, against the powers of
> this dark world and against the spiritual forces of evil in
> the heavenly realms. (Ephesians 6:12)

The high-ranking spirits, often called "territorial spirits," mentioned here are like military generals who command low-ranking demonic ground forces. As stated above, any attempt to defeat these demonic entities should *only be done* by intercessors who have much experience in these matters and are specially trained and called to this ministry, and only if given a specific assignment by God for such a task. To do otherwise violates the authority structure of heaven and lies beyond the spiritual domain of most individuals.

> As listed in Ephesians, the most authoritative of all de-
> monic atmospheres are the *powers and principalities.* . . .
> Through years of agreement by those living in the region,
> they have been given authority. To displace their power,
> Christians need to communicate with God and see his
> plans for the area. Of course, God always wants cities,

---

1. Jackson, *Needless Casualties of War*, 102. I also recommend Jackson's teaching at: https://www.youtube.com/watch?v=sRgGNmaQiZo

people, and regions delivered. However, going after a spiritual power outside of a person's realm of authority is not only unwise but unbiblical.[2]

2. De Silva and Liebscher, *Sozo*, 158.

PART EIGHT

A Word to Local Church
Pastors and Leaders

19

Leaders, You Need Intercessory Prayer

A PRAYER SHIELD IS a team of people whom a leader has individually invited to pray for him or her on a regular basis, for an extended period of time.[1]

Please don't stop reading!

Let's address the most common objections at the onset: there's something truly difficult about asking others to pray for you, especially to pray for you regularly.

It will make most leaders feel uneasy, unworthy, or unsafe.

It's too humbling.

It doesn't work.

And to each of these objections, I have respectfully said to many leaders over the years, "You've gotta get over it."

There is way too much to gain and way too much at stake to not make the effort to put together a team of people that you trust implicitly to pray for you, your family, and ministry.

And, if you recruit the right people (meaning people who are genuine intercessors and can keep confidentiality), you've ignited

---

1. Wagner, *Prayer Shield,*15. The term prayer shield refers to a team of intercessors who pray for the pastors and leaders in the church and ministry organizations.

some special people to do what God has gifted them to do as a part
of their unique and important Kingdom contribution.

WHY LEADERS NEED A PRAYER SHIELD

> The most underutilized source of spiritual power in our
> churches today is intercession for Christian leaders.[2]

While affirming that prayer changes things, Walter Wink, professor
emeritus at Auburn Theological Seminary in New York City says,
"It also changes what is possible for God."[3]

> God will do nothing on earth except in answer to believ-
> ing prayer. (John Wesley)[4]

Pastors and leaders in the church are at risk by virtue of the
fact that they're noticed in the spiritual realm and become targets
of the forces of darkness. If not to harm outright, a common enemy strategy is to neutralize a leader from doing ministry that is
anointed, powerful, and effective for the Kingdom.

As pastors and key leaders in the Church are taken down by
scandals and moral failure (which, sadly, happens too often), many
others become collateral damage, and the mission of the Church is
compromised for those in the Church as well as those looking for
yet another reason to disbelieve.

For better or for worse, leadership in the church comes with
greater responsibility and greater accountability to God as well as
the people that have been entrusted to their care.

> Not many of you should become teachers, my fellow
> believers, because you know that we who teach will be
> judged more strictly. (James 3:1)

Most leaders I know have few, if any, colleagues or close friends
with whom they feel safe, so they chose to live in virtual isolation.

---

2. Wagner, *Prayer Shield*, 19.
3. Wagner, *Prayer Shield*, 30.
4. Wagner, *Prayer Shield*, 29.

Isolated leaders are never a good thing and are easily targeted by the enemy to be attacked at their points of greatest vulnerability.

A PERSONAL CRISIS AND WAKE-UP CALL

I had been doing pastoral ministry vocationally for about ten years and was nearly three years into being the founding pastor of a church plant in Orange County, California.

It was during that season that my friend and spiritual mentor, James, suggested that I read C. Peter Wagner's book, *Prayer Shield*, then get a team organized as soon as possible.

I read the book but failed to follow through on recruiting a team of prayer folks (due to many of the same objections mentioned above). It was also during that same church-planting season that I received a call from my wife, telling me that I needed to rush to the hospital because our oldest son had an aortic aneurysm while at work and was being rushed into surgery. (I later learned from a friend who is an ER doctor that only one in a million survive the ordeal that he did.) While sitting with him in CCU only two days later, I received another call from my wife; she was taking one of our other sons to a different hospital because he was struggling with some severe emotional challenges.

Was the timing of it all just a coincidence?

Two days later, while sitting in my son's room in cardiac ICU (yes, he survived and is a miracle story at that hospital to this day), I sent a brief email to my spiritual mentor, James.

His response was direct, "Did you ever set up your prayer shield? If not, *do it now.*"

This time, I followed his direction.

Now I was angry. The enemy had made it personal.

PUTTING TOGETHER YOUR
PRAYER SHIELD TEAM

God has set up the rules for how things work in the spiritual realm in interaction with the natural realm.

For the most part, God in his wisdom and kindness has determined that he would do certain things *only in partnership* with his people.

I would encourage you to take some time to read the account of the Israelites' battle with the Amalekites in Exodus 17. See the relationship between prayer and the outcome of the battle. Moses' intercession (with the much-needed help of friends) is what released God's power on the battlefield and gave the Israelites their victory.

Rather than procrastinating in asking people to pray for you as I originally did, begin to prayerfully consider who you will ask to be to be a part of your prayer shield. You may wish to consider the following attributes for the people you will be asking:

1. They love to pray and will commit to pray for you regularly;
2. They understand the importance of confidentiality; deep character, maturity, and discipline of the intercessor is crucial and non-negotiable;
3. They won't have the expectation that you'll be praying equally for them; however, do pray for your intercessors and express gratitude when their prayers have been answered; and
4. Their intimacy with the Father and the satisfaction of doing what they are called to do is their reward.

> For even when I was in Thessalonica, you sent me aid more than once when I was in need. Not that I desire your gifts; what I desire is that more be credited to your account. I have received full payment and have more than enough. I am amply supplied, now that I have received from Epaphroditus the gifts you sent. They are a fragrant offering, an acceptable sacrifice, pleasing to God. (Philippians 4:16–18)

I encourage you to read Dr. Wagner's book.[5] As my own learning and understanding increased, I enthusiastically began sharing my experiences with anyone who would listen to me, especially those who were doing the work of ministry vocationally.

One of those people is April, a gifted colleague and a dear friend, who soon noticed some profound changes in her ministry

5. Wagner, *Prayer Shield,* 1992.

and personal life that were undeniable. She wrote about the notice-able impact that her prayer shield team was having on her life in a book that she wrote for pastors and lay leaders who do youth ministry across North America.

I conclude this section with a powerful quote from April's book with the hope that you'll do the same as she did:

> As you and I are sitting together and drinking an iced green tea or a nonfat latte, I'd strongly encourage you not to move forward in this brave endeavor until you've established an intercessor team to cover you, your family and your ministry in prayer. As you begin to push back on ground that the enemy has (temporarily) taken, you'll experience spiritual warfare and attacks. The enemy hates what we are looking to do. So to think that you can get away without having a strong backing of prayer is just foolish and proud.
>
> I was foolish and proud in this area for almost the first 15 years of my pastoral work. I occasionally asked people to pray with me and for me, but it was far from active and intentional. I didn't have any idea about the powers that are at work around my family and me as a result of the work I do. In the last couple of years, I've instituted a prayer shield of 15+ people who have a gift of intercessory prayer and are committed to pray for my ministry and family. I send them updates and requests; but predominantly they listen to God and pray according to the promptings of the Holy Spirit. I can honestly say my ministry is different as a result of these faithful warriors and teammates.[6]

---

6. Diaz, *Redefining the Role of the Youth Worker*, 41–42.

20

One Last Story: Forever Changed

OVERWHELMED? I KNOW. IT'S a lot to take in.

I've just shared an arsenal of tools to help equip your prayer ministry, and though we've covered a range of topics, let's remember the ultimate desired outcome of all of this:

Greater intimacy with God.

I leave you with a story of how prayer ministry, offered in a safe environment with safe leaders who are equipped with these tools, can help bring someone into deeper intimacy with our Heavenly Father.

One evening, after everyone was dismissed at the conclusion of a weekly prayer training session at church, a number of people hung around to visit, as usual. Amidst the flurry of people cleaning up and stacking chairs, I was approached by someone who noticed that "Joan," a lovely young woman who regularly attended these prayer training workshops, remained in her seat motionless, staring blankly into nothing, almost catatonic.

I came over to speak with her. There was no response whatsoever.

After about three tries, I heard a guttural, growling sound, emanating from her.

This confirmed that some sort of demonic oppression was at work against her, and that she needed to be prayed for and set free.

I asked one of the experienced prayer leaders to come and assist me. We gently escorted Joan to an adjacent room where we could meet with her in privacy. In an environment of safety, Joan began to open up and share for about ten minutes. We eventually learned that as a young girl, Joan had endured significant verbal trauma at the hands of the pastor of the church she attended with her mother. My heart sank, knowing that she had been wounded so deeply by someone who *should* have been a safe and protective person in her life.

The pastor's words had cursed her.

As a result, for over two decades, Joan would carry the anguish of spiritual abuse that not only wounded her emotionally, but also opened the door for the enemy to take advantage of an innocent girl. It wasn't until she was a young adult, loved and accepted in a community where she felt safe and free from judgement, that Joan could get the help she needed. Now, the Lord was providing an opportunity for Joan to engage her free will and participate in being set free.

I asked Joan if she would consider doing something that would require tremendous courage. Would she be willing to forgive the pastor for the terrible things he had said to her?

Without hesitation, bitterness, or resentment towards the pastor, Joan replied that she was ready to forgive him.

We walked Joan through a prayer of forgiveness, culminating in a word of blessing that she released for the pastor, his family, and his ministry.

Yes, Joan is a remarkable woman.

What followed next was a brief time of cleansing/deliverance prayer. Because Joan had freely forgiven her abuser, any claims or legal rights of the enemy to remain and oppress her were completely removed.

In the name, power, and authority of Jesus Christ, Joan was completely set free.

The radiance of her countenance was immediate evidence of her newfound freedom and deep-level healing.

Joan hasn't looked back on the past abuse or on that evening, when she gained new freedom. Instead, she has moved forward to what her Heavenly Father had in store for her all along. Later that same year, Joan was married to a wonderful man who loves Jesus—I had the extreme honor of officiating their wedding ceremony!

I live for these many opportunities, which have become a regular part of my life and ministry, to have a front-row seat to what our Father loves doing for his children, bringing them into deeper healing and wholeness.

I've found that he invites us to participate in what he is doing when we're willing to do the work of being safe people who cultivate safe spaces for prayer.

Remember the ultimate desired outcome of all this: greater intimacy with the Father.

NOW, YOUR JOURNEY BEGINS

In the introduction, my stated purpose for writing this book was a prayerful hope that you, dear reader, would do whatever it takes to participate and engage in prayer until prayer becomes normative in your ministry context.

As I come to the closing page, I am more convinced than ever that prayer is key. It is *God's invitation to participate in what he's doing, to live with him and partner with him at the intersection of the material and unseen realms.*

And now, I wish for you every blessing and God's favor as you do whatever he puts on your heart to do. May you experience the joy of walking in intimacy with your Father in heaven. And, may you accept many opportunities to have a front-row seat in partnership with what our kind and generous God does to bring encouragement, healing, and wholeness to the lives of people.

> Have I not commanded you? Be strong and courageous.
> Do not be afraid; do not be discouraged, for the Lord
> your God will be with you wherever you go. (Joshua 1:9)

Bibliography

Chambers, Oswald. *My Utmost for His Highest*. New York: Dodd, Mead and Co., 1963.

De Silva, Dawna, and Teresa Liebscher. *Sozo, Saved, Healed, Delivered: A Journey into Freedom with the Father, Son, and Holy Spirit*. Shippensburg, PA: Destiny Image, 2016.

Diaz, April. *Redefining the Role of the Youth Worker: A Manifesto of Integration*. San Diego: Oestreicher, 2013.

Eldredge, John. *Moving Mountains: Praying with Passion, Confidence, and Authority*. Nashville, Tennessee: Nelson, 2016.

Foster, Richard J. *Celebration of Disciplines*. San Francisco: Harper Collins, 1978.

Hill, Craig S. *Ancient Paths*. Littleton, Colorado: Family Foundations International, 1992.

———. *Power of a Parent's Blessing*. Lake Mary, Florida: Charisma, 2013.

Jackson, John Paul. *Needless Casualties of War*. Flower Mound, TX: Streams Ministries Int'l, 1999.

Otis, George, Jr. *Informed Intercession*. Ventura: Renew, 1999.

Wagner, C. Peter. *Prayer Shield: How to Intercede for Pastors, Christian Leaders and Others on the Spiritual Frontlines*. Ventura, CA: Regal, 1992.